Proclamation 4

Aids for Interpreting
the Lessons of the Church Year

Advent/ Christmas

Arland J. Hultgren

Series A

FORTRESS PRESS   **MINNEAPOLIS**

PROCLAMATION 4
Aids for Interpreting the Lessons of the Church Year
Series A: Advent-Christmas

Library of Congress Cataloging-in-Publication Data

(Revised for vol. 1–3, Series A)

Proclamation 4.

    Consists of 24 volumes in 3 series designated A, B, and C, which correspond to the cycles of the three year lectionary. Each series contains 8 basic volumes with the following titles: [1] Advent-Christmas, [2] Epiphany, [3] Lent, [4] Holy Week, [5] Easter, [6] Pentecost 1, [7] Pentecost 2, and [8] Pentecost 3. (In addition there are four volumes on the lesser festivals.)
    By Christopher R. Seitz and others.
    Includes bibliographies.
    1. Bible—Liturgical lessons, English. 2. Bible—Homiletical use. 3. Bible—Criticism, interpretation, etc. 4. Common lectionary. 5. Church year. I. Seitz, Christopher R. II. Title: Proclamation four.
BS391.2.S37   1988   264'.34   88–10982
ISBN 0-8006-4161-2 (Series A, Advent-Christmas).

Manufactured in the U.S.A.   AF 1–4161

93   92   91   90   89   1   2   3   4   5   6   7   8   9   10

Contents

The First Sunday in Advent

Lutheran	Roman Catholic	Episcopal	Common Lectionary
Isa. 2:1–5	Isa. 2:1–5	Isa. 2:1–5	Isa. 2:1–5
Rom. 13:11–14a	Rom. 3:11–14a	Rom. 13:8–14	Rom. 13:11–14
Matt. 24:37–44	Matt. 24:37–44	Matt. 24:37–44	Matt. 24:36–44

EXEGESIS

FIRST LESSON: ISAIAH 2:1–5. The lesson is located within a series of prophecies of Isaiah concerning Judah and Jerusalem (Isaiah 2–12). These prophecies, although edited in their present form at a later time, have been assigned to the last third of the eighth century B.C., when the Southern Kingdom (Judah was courting the favor of, and paying tribute to, Assyria. Syria and Israel waged war against Assyria (the so-called Syro-Ephraimite war, ca. 734–733), but Judah under King Ahaz refused to enter the coalition. In fact, Ahaz appealed to Tiglath–pileser of Assyria for protection against the coalition (cf. 2 Kings 16:5–9). During the same era Assyria invaded Israel, bringing the Northern Kingdom to an end (722 B.C.), and invaded Judah itself (701 B.C.), although the latter continued to exist independently. Isaiah the prophet, deeply committed to the Davidic royal tradition (9:7), was firmly set against alliances with Assyria (8:5–15) and, later on (705–701 B.C.), with Egypt (30:1–5).

The section opens with a superscription (2:1) introducing the material of chapters 2 through 12. This is followed by words of hope (2:2–4) and an appeal for a response (2:5). It is debated whether 2:2–5 reflects the actual preaching of Isaiah of Jerusalem or was composed after the destruction of Jerusalem and the temple (587 B.C.) or even in the postexilic era. The latter has been suggested on the grounds that the Jerusalem portrayed is idealized. It is also of interest that what appears in 2:2–4 is found almost verbatim in Mic. 4:1–3 as well. Its appearance in Micah (attributed to a younger contemporary of Isaiah) may also be due to editing in an exilic or postexilic setting.

The prophecy speaks of an eschatological hope ("the latter days"); yet it is a hope to be fulfilled in history. Speaking metaphorically, the temple mount in Jerusalem shall be the "highest of the mountains," that is, it will have preeminence on earth. All the nations shall flow to it. Again, the

5

language is figurative. The theme of the nations in procession to Zion is set forth also in Deutero- and Trito-Isaiah (40–66; see 45:14–23; 60:3–18; 61:5–7; 66:18–23). By such imagery the author speaks of all the nations of the world coming at last to seek the knowledge of God that Israel itself has. These nations will come under God's rule so that God's rule encompasses the world and there is worldwide peace. The Lord will teach the Lord's ways by means of the "law" (Torah, i.e., instruction) and "word," which comes out of the new Jerusalem (2:3). The picture is that of a theocracy without the need of priest, prophet, or scribe to mediate between God and the peoples of the world. Further, God will "judge between the nations" (2:4), that is, settle disputes among them. The instruments of warfare (swords and spears) will no longer be needed for settling disputes; indeed, they will be abandoned and transformed into farming implements. The section closes with an appeal to the "house of Jacob" to respond in obedience and trust in God so that the hope expressed might be fulfilled. Israel itself therefore must come under God's rule first; only then can the hope of all nations coming under God's rule be realized as well.

SECOND LESSON: ROMANS 13:11–14. The lesson comes from the hortatory section of Romans, which begins at 12:1 and runs through 15:13. The exhortations of this section presuppose what Paul has set forth in earlier portions of the letter, particularly those passages in which he speaks of the work of God in Christ for human redemption (e.g. 3:21–28) and the new life believers have in Christ (5:1—8:39). Within the hortatory section itself, Paul has exhorted his readers, among other things, to avoid haughtiness (12:3, 16), to put their varied gifts to proper use in the body of Christ (12:4–8), to refrain from vengeance (12:17–21), to conduct themselves as good citizens (13:1–7), and above all to practice love (12:9; 13:8–10).

The exhortation breaks off, and 13:11–12a is a statement concerning eschatological urgency. The Greek term behind "hour" (RSV) in 13:11 is *kairos,* which designates an appointed time of divine action (cf. 3:26; 5:6, etc.). The verse can be translated: "and furthermore, you know the time *(kairos),* that the hour is already here for you to wake from asleep." (Curiously, the RSV has "hour" for *kairos* and "full time" for *hōra* in the Greek text; the NIV provides a more literal translation at this point.) The implication is that the readers are asleep, a metaphor for being unresponsive to God. It is doubtful that Paul considered the Roman Christians to be such, however, since he has already said that they know the time. The metaphor fits with the imagery he uses in 12a: "The night is advanced, and the day is at hand." Here, along with the statement that "salvation is nearer to us now than when we first believed," Paul makes one of his most explicit utterances concerning eschatological expectation. Salvation is spoken of as future (as also at Rom. 5:9–10; 10:9; 1 Cor. 5:5). Elsewhere it is spoken of as having been accomplished as well (Rom. 8:24). What Paul has in mind is that, although believers have been saved by God's act in Christ, the fullness of salvation is future, and that with each passing day believers are closer to it. The night is still present (corresponding to the present age that is passing away; cf. 1 Cor. 2:6; 7:29–31; 10:11; Gal. 1:4), but the day of salvation has begun to dawn with Easter (1 Cor. 15:20–23; 2 Cor. 5:17).

In 13:12b–14 Paul resumes his exhortation. Believers, who belong to Christ already, are to "cast off the works of darkness and put on the armor of light"; that is, believers must reject wickedness (illustrated in 13:13) and be clothed with that protection which comes from God ("the weapons of our warfare are not worldly but have divine power," 2 Cor. 10:4). The conduct of believers is to be appropriate ("as in the day"). It is debatable whether the "day" means the day of the Lord's coming or is simply metaphorical for what honorable persons do in the day. Yet the distinction collapses. It is first of all metaphorical, but the day of salvation is at hand since the resurrection of Jesus from the dead. The vices listed are illustrative of the "works of darkness" to be rejected. The exhortation to Christians to put on Christ (13:14) seems at first to be inconsistent with the claim that the baptized "have put on Christ" (Gal. 3:27) already. Yet the life of the believer is a constant battle of reclaiming that which is given in baptism. The "flesh" (human weakness and self–centeredness) must ever be contended with; it seeks to have its "desires" served, which are illustrated by Paul in Gal. 5:18–21.

GOSPEL: MATTHEW 24:36–44. The passage is located within the larger unit of Matt. 24:1—25:46, in which Jesus speaks of last things. His disciples have already asked concerning "the sign of [his] coming and the close of the age" (24:3). He has warned them about being led astray by imposters who herald either themselves or others as the Christ (24:5, 11, 23–26), and he has also spoken of the tribulations of the last time and the coming of the Son of man. His coming as the Son of man will be known to his disciples because it will be announced by his angels, who will also gather the elect (24:31). It is important in the meantime that the disciples remain faithful to him (24:13) whose "words will not pass away" (24:35).

The passage itself takes up the question of timing. The point is made that no one knows the time of the coming of the Son of man except God alone (24:36). Disciples do not know (24:42). In fact, his coming will be at an hour they do not expect (24:44). Therefore they are to be ready at all times for his coming. The passage thus speaks of Christology (Jesus is spoken of as Son of man and Lord), eschatology (the time of his coming as Son of man is indefinite), and discipleship (it is incumbent upon Jesus' followers to be ready for his coming as Son of man at all times).

The passage consists of several parts: (1) a saying about the coming of the Son of man (24:36); (2) three illustrative sayings (24:37–41); (3) an exhortation to watchfulness (24:42); (4) a third illustrative saying (sometimes called the parable of the nocturnal burglar, 24:43); and (5) an exhortation to readiness (24:44).

The first of the illustrative sayings (24:37–39) alludes to the story of Noah in Genesis 6—7. There is actually no moral judgment passed here upon the proverbial wickedness of the people in Noah's day (in contrast to 2 Pet. 2:5, where God "brought a flood upon the world of the ungodly"). Their "eating and drinking, marrying and giving in marriage," are normal activities. Rather, the story is used to illustrate peoples' ignorance and indifference to what God is about to do. Noah's entry into the ark should have been a prophetic sign of the impending divine visitation, but they gave no need. The flood came and swept them away. So too the coming of the Son of man will take place as a divine action, and most people will be taken by surprise. The other two illustrative sayings (24:40–41) portray men and women doing normal tasks (work in the field, grinding at the mill) at the time of the coming of the Son of man. The judgment upon them ("one is taken and one is left" in each instance) is not on the basis of their activities or apparent conduct—for there are no differences—but on the basis of the Son of man's own judgment of which persons belong to him. He acts in sovereign freedom to judge. It is implied that those who are taken (saved) are those who have confessed Jesus as Son of man and have followed him (cf. 19:28 and the Q saying, 10:32–33).

The saying about the nocturnal burglar who breaks into a house (24:43) has to do with the theme of watchfulness. If the details are pressed, it would mean that as the watchfulness of a householder prevents a burglar's intrusion so the watchfulness of disciples forestalls the coming of the Son of man. But of course that would be going too far. The point of comparison is that Jesus' disciples are not to be like the householder (unaware, inattentive) who lets his house get broken into by a thief. The coming of the Lord is compared to the coming of a thief at night elsewhere (1 Thess. 5:2; Rev. 3:3; 16:15), and that motif can be heard here as well.

HOMILETICAL INTERPRETATION

The Gospel readings set the tone for the four Sundays in Advent of Year A. The Gospel for the First Sunday points to the Parousia, the second coming of Christ. Those for the Second and Third Sundays focus on John the Baptist as the forerunner of the Messiah's first coming, and that for the Fourth anticipates the Nativity. Over the four Sundays in Advent there is a shift—not gradual, but dramatic—from the expectation of the consummation of history to preparation for the Nativity.

The future orientation of the First Sunday in Advent is prominent in all three lessons. It would seem wise for the preacher to stick with it. It will give way soon enough to preparation for the first coming of Christ—the adult Jesus of whom the Baptist speaks, and then the baby born at Bethlehem.

FIRST LESSON: ISAIAH 2:1–5. This text sets forth an eschatological hope. Although its author may well have expected its fulfillment in history, he does not say when that might be. The future is left open to God's action. Particularly striking are the kinds of actions the writer envisions and calls for—and their sequence: (1) God will bring the envisioned hope into being; (2) the nations will respond; and (3) in the meantime, Israel is exhorted to "walk in the light of the Lord" (2:5).

The hope envisioned has not yet been realized in its fullness. Warfare still goes on. Resources are used to build instruments of war rather than implements of universal peace and well–being. Yet, for Christian faith, the hope of Isaiah has been realized in part through the life, death, resurrection, and reign of Jesus Christ. Isaiah envisions the raising of the temple mount above all mountains and hills. So Jesus and his community are the new temple in typological interpretation within the New Testament: in Jesus and his proclamation of the kingdom, "something greater than the temple is here" (Matt. 12:6); and the Christian community is the "temple of God" (1 Cor. 3:16; 2 Cor. 6:16). Moreover, the nations have responded to the divine action. The curtain of the temple has been torn (Matt. 27:51), and gentiles (the terms for "nations" in both Hebrew and Greek can also be translated "gentiles") have been admitted to fellowship with God along with Jewish Christians, so that "the whole structure is joined together and grows into a holy temple of the Lord . . . a dwelling place of God in the Spirit" (Eph. 2:21–22). In consequence of this good news, an exhortation follows. In fact, it is the only exhortation the author gives to the people of God, and that is to walk in the light of the Lord, that is, to be obedient and cognizant of God's will. In our time that will mean that Christians are to get their own lives in order, living as persons obedient to God's will and as a community of faith and witness. The community is also a community of hope and responsibility. The promises of God have not been fulfilled in their entirety. But Christians, walking in the light of the Lord, know what God intends for the nations of the world.

Although they may not agree on the precise means to establish and maintain universal peace, they will be united in efforts to provide alternatives to the use of military power. The text sets forth an eschatological hope, but it should not be dismissed on that count as utopian, nor should its possibilities of realization be relegated to an otherworldly plateau. The sheer reading of this text prompts hopes for universal peace even within our own time and future. It is surely appropriate to think thoughts of peace and to work for it.

SECOND LESSON: ROMANS 13:11–14. The text relates well to the season. It contrasts light and darkness, day and night. As the days grow shorter in December, as darkness becomes more apparent in our lives, and as we already have the glow of Christmas on our minds, we light the first candle of the Advent wreath. We declare the good news that salvation is near. In fact, it has been given already in Jesus' death and resurrection for us. He has assumed our sin and guilt before God. We have been baptized into his death and shall therefore be united with him in his resurrection (Rom. 6:5). But as long as time lasts, we know ourselves to be weak, and salvation seems far off. Yet it is not far off! The salvation given in Christ comes upon us day to day and will arrive in its unambiguous fullness at life's end. Since that is so, "the day is at hand," and we should "cast off the works of darkness and put on the armor of light" (13:12). But how do we do that? By moral transformation? That would seem to follow, since Paul goes on to speak of how Christians should conduct themselves. Yet for Paul there is something prior to moral transformation. That is to realize (the "You know" of 13:11) the time in which one lives, that it is the time between the dawn of grace in the resurrection of Jesus and the full day of his coming again. And that realization is accomplished by laying claim to what one has in baptism: "put on the Lord Jesus Christ" (13:14). Paul is concerned first of all with identity (Who am I?), from which moral responsibility (What am I to do?) flows. Such a message needs to be heard in the church during this season. In the days of December to come there will be a swell of exhortations to do good as the year-end appeals from various charities and institutions come into the homes of parishioners via their mailboxes and the air waves, as advertisers prescribe how to make loved ones happy, and as wishes for a "Merry Christmas" are heard not as wishes but as expectations that ought to be fulfilled. Advent offers the possibility of restraint and release: restraint from rushing into holiday celebrations before their time, and release from expectations that cannot really be met in spite of our best efforts. It is the time of lighting the candles slowly—only one per week—and realizing that salvation is not far off, but given in Christ, whose we are by baptismal grace.

GOSPEL: MATTHEW 24:36–44. The little parable at the end of the story (24:43) is a good place to begin. It can be updated by contemporary illustrations. People install automatic light switches (timer lights) to turn lights on at night to ward off possible intruders while they are away from their homes. Business managers install expensive security systems. In rural areas it is customary to have powerful yard lights which flood entire farmyards with light and are even visible to airline passengers far above. These are all signs of vigilance. And, just as we can be watchful in this life to protect our homes and property, so we ought to be vigilant for the coming of the Lord. He will come at a time no one expects.

But what does it mean to be vigilant (or ready) for the Lord's coming? It does not mean to flee from the world, even if that were possible. Ordinary activities and duties can, and should, be carried out; men and women are expected to be about their daily tasks at the Lord's coming (24:40–41). In this respect there is no distinction between Christians and others. The real distinction must be found elsewhere, within the realm of the invisible, and that is faith and discipleship. These may well have a bearing on how one carries out daily activities, of course, but the point is that the activities themselves are not unambiguous outer signs of one's standing before God. Peter and Andrew left their nets to follow Jesus (4:18–20), and James and John left their father as well (4:22). But their tasks were specified in ways that those of most persons are not. For most of us, our tasks at hand—as well as our leisure—are arenas for service to God and our neighbor in the present.

A problem arises that cannot be avoided. Most persons today do not have a vivid expectation of the return of Christ. Does this mean that the message should be avoided? No. The belief that "he will come again to judge the living and the dead" belongs to the core and structure of Christian faith, even though the timing and manner of his coming are not, and should not be, specified. Furthermore, this belief gives Christian faith a note of urgency. It teaches us that we cannot postpone fulfilling our commitments— either to God or to other persons. Life teaches us soon enough that opportunities are lost by inaction, such as not expressing love or care, and then it is too late.

The text bears a note of judgment upon us. Am I vigilant? Am I ready for the Lord's coming? But is there any good news in it? Yes. The message of Christ's coming is not simply a warning; it is also a declaration that Christ will claim those whom he has redeemed. The one to come is Jesus, whom we know in the gospel story to be the friend of sinners.

The Second Sunday in Advent

Lutheran	Roman Catholic	Episcopal	Common Lectionary
Isa. 11:1–10	Isa. 11:1–10	Isa. 11:1–10	Isa. 11:1–10
Rom. 15:4–13	Rom. 15:4–9	Rom. 15:4–13	Rom. 15:4–13
Matt. 3:1–12	Matt. 3:1–12	Matt. 3:1–12	Matt. 3:1–12

EXEGESIS

FIRST LESSON: ISAIAH 11:1–10. Like the First Lesson for the previous Sunday, this is situated within a series of prophecies of Isaiah concerning Judah and Jerusalem (Isaiah 2–12). Whether it represents the preaching of Isaiah of Jerusalem (eighth century B.C.) is a matter of debate. Some interpreters discern an exilic or postexilic origin on the grounds that the Davidic dynasty is assumed to have been overthrown; yet it will be restored (hence the "stump of Jesse" from which a "shoot" shall come, 11:1).

The reading consists of three smaller units. The first (11:1–5) concerns the future king of David's line. The second (11:6–9) portrays the expected, even paradisiacal new age. And the third (11:10) speaks again concerning the future king and his universal significance.

If we take the prophecy as genuinely from Isaiah, the prophet anticipates a royal succession in Jerusalem in which the coming king will embody the royal ideals of Israel. If it is an exilic or postexilic piece, the writer anticipates a restoration of the Davidic dynasty through a king who embodies those ideals. In any case, the passage speaks of a descendant of Jesse, the father of David (cf. 1 Sam. 16:1–13), who will reign as king. Behind all of this stands the Davidic royal theology expressed in the promise of God through Nathan to David: "Your house and your kingdom shall be made sure for ever before me; your throne shall be established for ever" (2 Sam. 7:16; cf. Ps. 89:4, 29–36). Like David, upon whom "the Spirit of the Lord came mightily" at his anointing by Samuel (1 Sam. 16:13), so the ideal coming king will be endowed by the Spirit (11:2), by which he will have the gifts (or qualities) appropriate for his office. The qualities are traditional, although there may be nuances among them: "wisdom and understanding" for wise internal governance of the people, "counsel and might" for external diplomatic relationships, and "knowledge and fear of the Lord" for appropriate reverence and regard for the cultic life of the people. In terms of rendering judgment, the king will possess "righteousness" (11:4, 5). Helpful commentary on the meaning of a king's righteousness is provided by Ps. 72:1–8 (the Psalm for the Day): to "defend the cause of the poor, . . . give deliverance to the needy, and crush the oppressor" (72:4). According to Isaiah, the king will not be deceived by appearances or hearsay (11:3). He will vindicate the poor and the meek— those who are customarily bypassed by systems of justice (11:4a). And by judgments proceeding from his mouth ("the rod of his mouth," "the breath of his lips"), he will decide against the oppressors of the poor and meek (11:4b).

The future, idealized age portrayed in the next section (11:6–9) is, according to our present text from Isaiah, a consequence of the future king's reign, a messianic era. The reign of the Lord's anointed has cosmic significance (cf. Ps. 72:3, 16). Natural enemies in the animal world—both wild and domestic—will live together in peace (11:6–7). Even poisonous snakes will be no threat to helpless children (the "suckling child" and "weaned child," 11:8). The final verse of this section (11:9) recapitulates the picture of peace: the "holy mountain" is metaphorical for the place of God's presence (cf. Exod. 15:17), which will be the entire world; this peace will be established by knowledge of the Lord throughout "the earth."

The last verse of our reading (11:10) speaks of the universal significance of the messianic king: he will be as "an ensign" to "the peoples," whom the "nations" will seek. Paul alludes to this passage as having its fulfillment in Christ at Rom. 15:12 (see the Second Lesson).

SECOND LESSON: ROMANS 15:4–13. The reading comes at the close of a section in Romans where Paul discusses relationships between the "strong" and "weak" (14:1—15:13). Who are these persons? Those labeled "weak" are vegetarians by religious convictions (14:2); they observe certain days (14:5–6); and they refrain from wine (14:21). The "strong" do not have such scruples, and Paul includes himself among them (15:1). Both groups are considered to be Christians by Paul, even if the former are called "weak in faith" (14:1). Commentators have offered several suggestions concerning these groups. Essentially, however, the main distinction between them is that the "weak" are Christians who observe ceremonial customs derived from a strict reading of the Old Testament and Jewish tradition (cf. Dan. 1:12, 16 on vegetarianism, and Num. 6:2–3 on the Nazarite view of abstinence from wine). The "strong," on the other hand, consider themselves freed from the observance of ceremonial law through Christ, who is the end of the law (10:4). But Paul maintains that the strong ought not despise or even pass judgment on the weak (14:3, 10, 13). In fact, they ought to restrain themselves from exercising their own freedom if and when it offends the weak (14:13–15, 10).

Apart from this larger context, the passage assigned—when read by itself—starts abruptly. The first verse (15:4) depends on the preceding one, which contains a quotation from Ps. 69:9, and which Paul interprets christologically to speak of Jesus' humiliation. This verse from Scripture, Paul says, speaks to Christians in the present as well (cf. a similar expression in 1 Cor. 9:10), and he draws out the implications in 15:5–6. Above all, that is to live in "harmony" (RSV), or literally, to "think the same among one another in accord with Christ Jesus" (15:5). It is not likely that Paul meant by this that one side (weak or strong) should abandon its position or that both should seek a compromise of convictions (which would be impossible). Instead, he must mean that both sides should be of the same mind in giving respect and regard for one another, which would be in accord with the mind and manner of Christ regarding all. The intent of this is expressed in a purpose clause (15:6): that there be unity among both weak and strong in their praise of God.

At 15:7 Paul uses again the imperative verb that stands at the beginning of the section (14:1): "welcome" (RSV), "accept" (NEB), or "receive." The congregation as a whole is admonished to be receptive, but Paul must have the strong in mind especially (as at 14:1). And this imperative is founded on the indicative: "as Christ has welcomed you" (cf. 14:3). If Paul has particular persons in mind at Rome, the "strong" must have included not only persons like himself (cf. 15:1), of Jewish background, but gentile Christians as well. It is precisely the latter, then, that Paul addresses in 15:8–9. Christ became a servant to the Jews; those very persons now being called "weak" are part and parcel of the people to whom God's faithfulness has been demonstrated, and in whom the patriarchal promises have been confirmed. And only because of that have the Scriptures been fulfilled concerning gentile praise of God. Paul quotes four passages from the Old Testament (Ps. 18:49; Deut. 32:43; Ps. 117:1; Isa. 11:10) that speak of gentile praise and worship of God. The last of these passages (contained in our First Lesson) is particularly apt in context, for it speaks of the Messiah of Israel as the one in whom gentiles have hope. The section closes with a wish for the joy and peace that come from faith in Christ. The outcome of such joy and peace through believing is abounding in hope "by the power of the Holy Spirit." The verse can hardly be reduced to a syllogism. Paul's point is that the true fruits of faith and the Spirit are joy, peace, and hope. These overcome all distinctions between weak and strong.

GOSPEL: MATTHEW 3:1–12. The reading inaugurates a new section of the Gospel of Matthew. The genealogy and infancy narratives (1:1—2:23) have been concluded; what follows are accounts of John the Baptist, Jesus' baptism by John, the temptation in the wilderness, and Jesus' early ministry in Galilee (3:1—4:25). Matthew 3:1–12 focuses on John the Baptist and his preaching. For Matthew, this person is the forerunner of the Messiah; he signifies the return of Elijah promised in Mal. 4:5–6: "He is Elijah who is to come" (Matt. 11:14; cf. also 17:9–13).

The passage contains three smaller units. In the first (3:1–6), where John is introduced, Matthew draws heavily on Mark 1:2–6, although he rearranges the material and alters it somewhat. That is seen immediately at 3:2. According to Mark 1:4, John was "preaching a baptism of repentance for the forgiveness of sins." Matthew places the preaching of John into direct discourse: "Repent, for the kingdom of heaven is at hand." Two items stand out in particular: (1) the message of John is identical to that of Jesus at 4:17; and (2) although John preaches repentance, Matthew does not say that forgiveness of sins follows as a consequence. Matthew reserves forgiveness of sins for Jesus alone (26:28)—and then for his disciples after him in the post-Easter church (9:8; 18:18). Therefore it appears that Matthew has altered the material to underscore John's place as forerunner of the one who grants forgiveness of sins. At 3:3 Matthew (like Mark before him) quotes Isa. 40:3 in its Septuagintal form (cf. the Hebrew text: "A voice cries: 'In the wilderness prepare the way of the Lord, make straight in the desert a highway for our God.' "). John is described in the likeness of Elijah (cf. 2 Kings 1:8). Concerning those who respond to John's preaching, Matthew adds to Mark's roll call (the people of Judea and Jerusalem) those of "the region about the Jordan" as well.

The meaning of John's baptism can be understood in light of ancient Jewish proselyte baptism. When gentiles were received into membership in the Jewish community, they (both men and women) were baptized (and males were also circumcised), signifying a ritual cleansing. But John the Baptist, according to our Gospel accounts, called not gentiles but Jews themselves to repent, confess their sins, and be baptized in preparation for the coming reign of God. The note of judgment can be heard in this: the people of Israel are regarded in the same way as gentiles—unclean in the eyes of God. By means of his baptism and his call to repentance (meaning "to return"), he summons the people of Israel to return to covenant fidelity to God in preparation for his reign, which is drawing near.

In the second unit (3:7–10), concerning John's preaching of repentance, Matthew draws from Q material (cf. Luke 3:7–9). The wording is almost identical to that of Luke, although Matthew has "many of the Pharisees and Sadducees coming for baptism" over against Luke's "the multitude coming to be baptized by him." Matthew, but not Luke, has made the change from Q (for two other instances where Matthew has "Pharisees and Sadducees" when his sources do not, see 16:1, 6 over against Mark 8:11, 15). By making the change, Matthew targets the especially pious of Israel. He addresses them as a "brood of vipers"—which for Matthew signifies that they are evil (cf. 12:34; 23:33)—who are fleeing from the wrath to come (the final judgment; cf. 1 Thess. 1:10). He calls upon them to "bear fruits that befit repentance." The bearing of good fruit by the faithful is stressed elsewhere by Matthew (7:16–20; 12:33), and it appears again in this text (3:10). Physical descent from Abraham does not count as sufficient readiness for the coming reign of God (3:9). By so saying, John discredits Israel's election; the people of Israel are regarded once again as gentiles have been. Judgment is taking place "even now," John says (3:10), as though the final judgment is merely a certification of what takes place in his ministry, as people are confronted with the last opportunity to repent and bear good fruit.

The third unit (3:11–12), concerning John's preaching of the Messiah's coming, is based on Q material as well (cf. Luke 3:16–17). The most notable thing here is the contrast between two baptisms. John's baptism with water is symbolic of repentance, of dying and then rising to new life, turning from an old path to a new one. But the Messiah will baptize "with the Holy Spirit and with fire." Is this an allusion to Pentecost with its manifestation of the Spirit and tongues of fire (Acts 2:1–4)? More likely it alludes to the advent of the Messiah and his purification of Israel. The coming of the Spirit was anticipated with the arrival of the messianic age (cf. Joel 2:28), and fire is a means of cleansing (cf. Amos 7:4; Mal. 3:2). With the coming of the Messiah, the time of preparation will have been spent. He will carry out divine judgment, which is portrayed in the act of threshing (3:12). In all of this, one, not two, advents of the Messiah is anticipated. The Messiah will come, judge, and create a purified community.

HOMILETICAL INTERPRETATION

FIRST LESSON: ISAIAH 11:1–10. We picture in our minds the stump of a tree that has been cut down. The stump has remained for some time, perhaps a year or two, but it is not dead. The energies of life are astir even yet. And out of its side, or from down in its roots, a shoot grows tall before us. It is a picture familiar to most who have observed trees and shrubs cared for by human hands.

The imagery is parabolic about God and the Messiah. The Davidic succession upon the throne was put to an end. A great tree had been felled; only the stump remained. But the prophet anticipates a new day due to the divine, life-giving energies at work. From David's family a shoot or branch will rise, a person who will be greater than all his predecessors. He will possess all the qualities expected of a king; he will be just in judgment; and his kingdom will be one in which natural enemies are at peace—the lion and the lamb, and so on. (If this is so in the animal kingdom, how much more will it be with people!)

For Christian faith, the one expected by Isaiah and others as the messianic king is Jesus of Nazareth. The objection can be raised that, since there is no universal peace, the Messiah has not come, and therefore Jesus was/is not the Messiah. To this the response can be given that the Messiah has indeed appeared in Jesus' life, death, and resurrection. He is that shoot or branch that has sprung forth from David's family. Indeed he too was cut down, crucified on a tree and put in a tomb. But due to the divine, life-giving energies at work, he was raised from death. He is righteous, and he establishes peace among persons who come under his dominion. This dominion is universal, encompassing people throughout the world. Every Christian has been called to follow Jesus into the ways of peace with others, and has opportunities for the making of peace in the wider world. The perfection anticipated by our text is of course eschatological. But like the text from Isa. 2:1–5 for the previous Sunday, this one too prompts hopes for universal peace, confirms that it is God's will, and encourages us to work toward it in our time and in the future.

SECOND LESSON: ROMANS 15:4–13. Undoubtedly, it is on account of 15:12 ("The root of Jesse shall come. . ."), which picks up lines from our First Lesson, that this passage is assigned for a Sunday in Advent. But the passage is fitting for the season also in its reference to Christ as the one who came among us as "a servant to the circumcised . . . to confirm the promise given to the patriarchs, and . . . that the Gentiles might glorify God" (15:8–9). The words recall the song of Simeon (the Nunc Dimittis) concerning Christ as "a light for revelation to the Gentiles, and for glory to thy people Israel" (Luke 2:32).

As pointed out in the Exegesis, the passage in context has to do primarily with relationships between the "weak" and "strong," but this issue is not apparent when beginning the reading at 15:4. One should ask before preaching on this text whether it is necessary to provide the background information in a sermon. It seems that some such information would be helpful, and then the thrust of the sermon could be on the handling of conflicting pieties within the church in light of the Advent hope.

Christians differ in piety and practice, and that has been so from the very beginning of· the church. Romans 14 and 15 show that differences existed in the church at Rome in Paul's day. Legitimate differences can exist among Christians without mutually writing each other off as non-Christian. Paul regarded both the "weak" and the "strong" as Christians. He did not ask people to abandon their positions or compromise their convictions but, nevertheless, to give respect to one another and to live in such harmony that there is unity in worship and the service of Christ. In short, the love Christians share for Christ and for one another must, in the end, outweigh the principles that divide them. Christian love *(agapē)* includes willful respect or regard for the other person. It is a regard that wishes for the other all the good one wishes for oneself (as in the golden rule of Matt. 7:12). It is not simply a matter of liking the other person to a high degree; it is not simply a matter of feeling. It is a matter of commitment to the neighbor, as expressed in 15:2.

Differences in piety become more apparent as the mobility of the population increases and as people are influenced by a host of factors (the media, experiences with friends, relatives, or spouses of different denominations, etc.). These differences are communicated only in part by code words of our time, such as "high church," "low church," "evangelical," "confessional," "conservative," "liberal," "spirituality," and so on. There are those who obtain "spiritual directors" for consultations on a regular basis. There are those for whom discipleship in the world is the only appropriate piety.

Though such differences exist and are very real, the worship of the church is to be of one voice, according to Paul (15:6). People of differing pieties, in his view, can and ought to make common confession and praise of God. The corporate has precedence over the private. The congregation gathers to hear the Word of God and to celebrate the Eucharist. It is God's Word and the Lord's Table that should set the agenda and, like twin engines, provide the energy and thrust of worship.

Advent is a time of expectation. Our lesson speaks four times of hope (15:4, 12, twice in 13), and hope in the New Testament sense means expectation, not wish. Hope here is not simply optimism (hope in general) but hope in God's salvation. That is why God is called the "God of hope" (15:13). Here we hear (and the sermon should proclaim) the gospel, the good news of God's saving work in Christ. God has acted in Christ to fulfill his promises to Israel, which included the promise that there will be a place for the gentiles in God's kingdom. If God's saving work is for all the world—with its richly woven fabric of different voices, languages, and cultures—the congregation, on a smaller scale, should be able to accommodate differences within itself and be one in its worship of God.

GOSPEL: MATTHEW 3:1–12. Alex Haley touched a responsive chord with the publication of his book *Roots* (Garden City, N.Y.: Doubleday & Co., 1976), which was also the basis for a highly influential television miniseries. Many people were inspired by this to search for their own roots. Genealogical research has become a popular pastime for many people. It seems that the search for their roots is a quest for their own identity. The assumption is that one's own character and ways are rooted and shaped to some degree by one's own genetic and ethnic past. And if I am unsure about my character and ways, I might find some clues in my ancestors about what these are likely to be.

In matters of faith it is easy to become smug on the basis of our roots, our ancestors in the faith—who may go back many generations, even centuries. But John the Baptist's words to his contemporaries in 3:9 speak to us. We should not presume to speak (or think) about the fidelity of our ancestors as accruing to our credit, for "the axe is laid to the root" (3:10). Roots do not count. Each of us stands before God as an individual.

John appears as the forerunner of the Messiah. The Messiah, he says, will come to judge. It is necessary then that persons prepare for his coming. They cannot rely on their spiritual heritage but, rather, must repent and bear good fruits (3:8, 10). The importance of bearing good fruits is also set forth in 7:16–20 and 12:33. The point is that the character and ways of persons, like trees and their fruits, ought to be consistent—and consistently good. The saying of Luther is fitting here: "Good works do not make a [person] good, but a good [person] does good works" ("person" substituted for "man" in the text quoted from Martin Luther, "A Treatise on Christian Liberty," in *Three Treatises* [Philadelphia: Muhlenberg Press, 1943], 271).

John anticipates the Messiah's coming. We anticipate his coming again in glory, but we know him as Jesus, who has already come. He came to baptize with the Spirit and fire in order to create a purified and renewed humanity. Christians belong to that new humanity today, even though they live in the old world. Repentant and baptized, Christians live lives that bear the good fruits of the kingdom of God. What these good fruits will be cannot be specified in advance of their appearance, but they will emerge from persons who are devoted to Christ and who exercise love for others.

To return to our roots metaphor, Advent is a time to become more deeply rooted in Christ. Through repentance and faith in Christ, being rooted in him, believers are as trees that are good, that bear good fruits in the world.

The Third Sunday in Advent

Lutheran	Roman Catholic	Episcopal	Common Lectionary
Isa. 35:1–10	Isa. 35:1–6a, 10	Isa. 35:1–10	Isa. 35:1–10
James 5:7–10	James 5:7–10	James 5:7–10	James 5:7–10
Matt. 11:2–11	Matt. 11:2–11	Matt. 11:2–11	Matt. 11:2–11

EXEGESIS

FIRST LESSON: ISAIAH 35:1–10. The lesson is taken from the so-called Little Apocalypse of Isaiah (Isaiah 34–35), which is judged by major scholars to have been composed in the postexilic era. The contents of 35:10 (the return of the redeemed to Zion) speak in favor of such a view. Some have suggested that these two chapters are dependent upon the prophecies of Isaiah 40–55 (Deutero-Isaiah), since they share words, imagery, and themes with the latter. While Isaiah 34 has to do with judgment upon the nations (34:1–4), and particularly upon Edom (34:5–17), chapter 35 envisions the restoration of Judah and Zion (35:10) through divine blessing upon the land and people.

Portions of the passage speak of the transformation of the wilderness (35:1–2, 6b–7) and the strengthening and healing of persons in need of help (35:3–6a), but all of this is for a specific purpose: that the "ransomed of the Lord shall return, and come to Zion" (35:10). In short, creation (or new creation) is in service of redemption. It is a matter of creative redemption, by which God opens up for God's people a way for salvation. Commentators generally consider the "ransomed of the Lord" to be, in this context, Jews of the Diaspora, not simply those Jews living in Babylon. Diaspora Jews have already been referred to at 11:12 and 27:12–13.

The wilderness and dry land will be transformed into a luxuriant garden, a virtual paradise (35:1–2), including majestic forests (Lebanon) and verdant pastures (Carmel and Sharon). To the weak and fearful there is the exhortation to be strong and to trust in God, who is coming to save (35:3–4). At this point follow the eschatological promises of the healing of the blind, the deaf, the lame, and the mute (35:5–6a). These disabilities are envisioned as being removed altogether in the time of salvation.

The theme of the transformation of the wilderness is again resumed in 35:6b–7. This time the imagery is more clearly focused on the coming forth of water in abundance. It is based in part on Deutero-Isaiah: for "streams in the desert," see 43:19; for "the burning sand shall become a pool," see 41:18. The transformation provides those returning to Jerusalem with plentiful water for their journeys.

The passage closes with a vision concerning "the Holy Way" to Zion (35:8–10), based in part on the imagery of 40:3. This way, now understood to be like a garden and with abundant water, will be free of danger from wild animals, and it will also be free of persons not worthy to take it (the "unclean" and "fools"). But the "redeemed" (i.e., those set free from captivity) will come to Zion with "singing" and "joy." The opposites ("sorrow and sighing," stated in reverse, or chiastic, order) will disappear.

The writer of the passage thus envisions a glorious future for God's covenant people. This future is idealized; it is a messianic age to be inaugurated by God. The world is transformed, the downcast and fearful are strengthened, the disabled are healed, and there is perfect communion between God and God's people—an age of joy and gladness. It is an age projected into the future, but whether the writer thought that it would be fulfilled in history is not clear. The passage—taken together with chapter 34 (see esp. 34:4)—has therefore been judged to border on apocalyptic, awaiting fulfillment beyond the course of history.

SECOND LESSON: JAMES 5:7–10. The Greek word *parousia* occurs twice in this passage (5:7, 8). *Parousia* can mean "presence" (cf. 2 Cor. 10:10), but more frequently the word refers to the second coming of Christ in glory (Matt. 24:3; 1 Cor. 15:23; 2 Thess. 2:8; etc.). The latter is meant here.

The Epistle of James is generally judged by critical scholarship to have been composed in the last part of the first century. The James to whom it is attributed by tradition is probably James the brother of the Lord (mentioned in Mark 6:3 and Gal. 1:19), but in fact, we do not know who wrote it. Authorship by this James is not likely on the grounds that it was written in good Greek, that it speaks of the "law of liberty" (1:25; 2:12) and lacks the cultic legalism that characterized the outlook of the historical James (Gal. 2:12–13). Some interpreters have suggested that the book was originally a non-Christian Jewish writing, which was "Christianized" later by adding references to "Jesus Christ" (1:1; 2:1). If one adopts this view, the Parousia of the Lord would refer to the coming not of Jesus (as Lord), but God. Others, however, consider the book to have a Christian authorship. This seems to be more likely. Above all, the discussion of faith and works in 2:14–26 surely presupposes the writer's acquaintance with the teaching (or a caricature of the teaching) of the apostle Paul. Moreover, the discussion of the Lord's Parousia seems, in the final analysis, to refer to the coming of Christ in glory.

The letter contains 108 verses. Within these verses there are no less than fifty-four imperative verbs, and so the letter is primarily hortatory in tone. The passage under consideration here, only four verses in length, contains five imperatives in the Greek text. The passage is essentially an exhortation to patience, although that is relieved in 5:9 somewhat with the exhortation not to grumble.

Twice we hear the exhortation to "be patient" (5:7, 8), patient for the Lord's Parousia. New Testament writers address their readers regarding the Parousia in two distinct ways: (1) get ready for the Parousia of the Lord right now, for it is soon, and (2) be prepared to wait for the Lord's Parousia, for it is delayed. In this passage there are mixed signals. Along with the exhortations to patience—which seem to presuppose a delay—it is said that the Lord's Parousia is at hand (5:8b) and that the Judge is standing at the doors (5:9b). The two points of view, however, are not opposed to each other in a hortatory context. The promised imminent coming of the Lord is the basis for being patient. Readers are not to give up hope; they are to persevere and see their patience vindicated.

The saying about the farmer (5:7b) has text-critical problems. Some Greek texts can be translated "early and late rain" (as in the RSV; cf. NEB), but others as "early and late fruit" (with "he," the farmer, as subject of the clause), and still others as "early and late" (with no noun following). In fact, the best ancient witnesses have the last reading. Nevertheless, it is probably "early and late rain" that is meant ("early and late" being idiomatic for that meaning). The picture is that of a farmer who waits for his produce to appear, and that picture is the model of patience.

The verb translated "establish" in 5:8 can also be translated "strengthen." "Strengthen your heart" is a traditional expression in Judaism (cf. Judg. 19:4, 8) and then in Christianity (cf. 1 Thess. 3:13). It means to have one's heart firmly fixed, and here that would mean to have a resolute expectation concerning the Lord's coming. Grumbling against one another is prohibited (5:9). The "Judge" who stands at the doors could be God, but is more likely Christ (as in the imagery of Rev. 3:20). Finally, the writer appeals to the prophets (presumably of the Old Testament) as an example of "suffering and patience" for Christians in the present. They spoke "in the name of the Lord" but had to wait for the vindication of their messages.

GOSPEL: MATTHEW 11:2–11. The passage opens with the words: "And when Jesus had finished instructing his twelve disciples" (11:1). As at four other places in the central section of Matthew's Gospel (3:1—25:46) where similar phrases are used (7:28; 13:53; 19:1; 26:1), the verse serves notice that a transition is being made into a new narrative section. Just before this transition, Jesus' instructions for the twelve disciples had to do primarily with their mission, including how to conduct themselves and what to expect in the way of persecution (10:1–42). But now the narrative resumes (11:1—12:50). Jesus is still in Galilee, and he teaches and preaches in unspecified Galilean cities.

The lesson consists of two major units. The first (11:2–6) presents a question from John and a response by Jesus. The material can be assigned to Q (cf. Luke 7:18–23). John is not certain whether Jesus is the Christ (of course the phrase "deeds of the Christ" in 11:2 reflects the estimate of the narrator Matthew, not John). He sends his question by way of his disciples (that John had disciples is attested not only in the passages mentioned, and their parallels, but also in John 1:35; 3:25). The description of the Messiah as the "Coming One" (11:3) is not common (cf. Matt. 21:9 and parallels; Heb. 10:37), but it is based on Old Testament passages (Ps. 117:26; Hab. 2:3). In any case, the reply of Jesus is to give neither a direct yes or no to the question whether he is the one to come. What is happening, however, is evidence that the kingdom is breaking in upon the world. That which Isaiah envisioned in his prophetic oracles (26:19; 29:18–19; 35:5–6; 61:1) is now taking place. Whoever perceives the connections and concludes that Jesus does the work of the Coming One is blessed (11:6).

The second unit (11:7–11), also from Q (cf. Luke 7:24–28), relates Jesus' words concerning John. Jesus asks the crowds three questions about their estimate of him (11:7–9). The point of the three questions is to drive home the fact that the people went out to see a prophet (11:9). Indeed, John is "more than a prophet" in that he had a superior role: to be the herald of the Messiah's coming, preparing his way. He is the messenger promised by the last of the prophets (Mal. 3:1 is quoted), even Elijah who is to come (11:14, alluding to Mal. 4:5). John is extolled as the greatest of human beings (11:11a). Yet there are persons even greater (11:11b)! How can this be? They are greater in the sense that, while John stood before the coming of the kingdom, the disciples of Jesus (even the least of them) stand within it.

HOMILETICAL INTERPRETATION

FIRST LESSON: ISAIAH 35:1–10. The prophet speaks of divine action and human response, and both are envisioned in the future. The Lord will come to save his people (35:4), giving sight to the blind, hearing to the deaf, healing to the lame, and speech to the mute (35:5–6). And those who are saved will respond with joy and gladness (35:10).

The healing actions mentioned are recounted in part within the Gospel for the Day (Matt. 11:5) concerning the ministry of Jesus: "The blind receive their sight and the lame walk . . . and the deaf hear." That which the writer of Isaiah 35 envisions has therefore been enacted in the ministry of Jesus. Various accounts in the Gospels portray Jesus as healing the blind (Mark 10:46–52), the deaf (7:31–37), the lame (Matt. 15:30–31; 21:14), and the mute (Mark 7:31–17; 9:14–29).

To notice such connections between Isaiah and the ministry of Jesus, as portrayed in the Gospels—and to speak of them in preaching—is theologically legitimate. Informed by modern biblical criticism, we can agree that the writer of Isaiah 35 did not have Jesus of Nazareth and his ministry in mind while composing his lines. Yet he expressed a hope, even a promise, which was fulfilled in the healing ministry of Jesus. One can object that not all that was promised—the healing of all the blind and so forth, and the transformation of nature—was fulfilled. But the imagery of prophetic and apocalyptic expectation is to be taken as suggestive and figurative, not literally. There are sufficient links to see connections from a faith perspective. And there is more yet to come with the Parousia of Christ. Then we expect perfect healing and the transformation of the world.

Advent is a season of expectation. In 35:3–4 there is a prescription for those who await the future coming of the Lord. Because of our expectation of his coming, we are summoned by God's Word to be strong and fearless. We do not face a future that is empty, as though the history of the cosmos is an interlude of sights and sounds enclosed by a dark silence of nothingness. The summons to be strong and fearless can be especially urgent in a world where nihilism on the one side and apocalyptic resignation on the other either deny God's very existence or else speak of a God who destroys the creation except for a few who are elected for salvation. Be strong and of good courage! Care for the earth; care for those who suffer; seek a better world in history's future. We have a vision of history's outcome, given by this passage of Scripture and in the gospel of the risen Christ. In the meantime, Christians seek to see that outcome mirrored as much as possible in the time before the end.

SECOND LESSON: JAMES 5:7–10. As does the previous text (Isa. 35:3–4), this one calls upon its hearers to muster strength: "Establish your hearts, for the coming of the Lord is at hand" (5:8). It also exhorts them to patience (5:7, 8).

One should reflect on whether this passage can be the basis for a sermon (especially in a congregation of Reformation heritage!). It is from James; it exhorts people to patience and strength of heart (can exhortation give space for the gospel?); and it does not have a very Christmas-like character, and Christmas is getting close.

To be sure, a sermon on the themes of patience and strength of heart could be simply hortatory and moralistic, devoid of the gospel. Yet, on the other hand, it is fitting to explore these good, sturdy biblical themes in light of the gospel, which the Season of Advent provides for admirably well. It reminds us that times of waiting upon God are a part of life, and that the waiting is good—like the waiting for a loved one at the airport or train station—because we know and love the God for whom we wait.

As these words are being written, it is the summer of 1988, a season of growing. However, vast sections of the United States are experiencing the worst drought since the Dust Bowl days of the 1930s. "Behold, the farmer waits for the precious fruit of the earth, being patient over it until it receives the early and the late rain" (5:7). There is no alternative to waiting. There is nothing one can do. In many parts of the country the summer of '88 will be remembered for a long time as a time of trial. For all of us it can be a reminder that even though we seem to have abundant resources and the best technology in the world, and even though we like to think that the future holds unlimited possibilities, life is not in our own hands after all. It is a gift. Lack of rain can undo all projections of expected yields from the fields.

If waiting with patience is sometimes necessary in the obvious spheres of our lives, so it is in our relationship with God. Although the Savior has come, we look forward to celebrating his incarnation, and we look finally to his coming in glory. Christians, however, are as liable as anyone else to value the immediate and the tangible. This can be seen even in worship practices where the focus shifts away from the objective character of worship (the adoration of God in light of the biblical drama) to a desire and propensity to ventilate one's subjective feelings, and so worship gives way to religious programming designed to please the "audience." But this text from James reminds us that the biblical drama is not yet finished. In fact, we are enclosed within its outer limits, the horizon of its future. Our adoration should continue to be fixed on God who shall bring all things to their completion, "for the coming of the Lord is at hand," and "the Judge is standing at the doors" (5:8–9).

Yes, there is exhortation. Yes, there is gospel. The good news is that God has sent God's Son for the salvation of the world. And to be exhorted to patience and strength of heart—while it is a command—is also good, because it communicates the certainty that God will restore and refashion the creation, the kingdom will come, and God's people will enjoy the salvation God brings.

GOSPEL: MATTHEW 11:2–11.   In the Gospel for the previous Sunday (Matt. 3:1–12) we heard the stirring words of John at the Jordan River concerning the one who is to come. The Messiah will baptize with the Spirit and fire, and he will exercise judgment. His coming will be dramatic, to say the least.

But Jesus does not really fit the mold. He comes on the scene as one who proclaims the kingdom of God, calls upon people to trust in God, heals the sick, and befriends tax collectors and persons labeled "sinners." It is little wonder that John questions whether Jesus is the one to come or not. Jesus fits neither John's expectations nor those of Jewish messianism in general. The question of 11:3 is totally understandable.

The response of Jesus is to portray messiahship in a new way. One does not find in the Old Testament and other ancient Jewish sources the thought that the Messiah would do those things listed in 11:4–6. Yet, insofar as Jesus speaks here of the Messiah at all, he does not create a picture unrelated to the sources, for the words of 11:4–6 are straight out of the Scriptures of Israel, and they speak of the blessings of the messianic age, which include both healing and good news to the poor. One finds both connections and fractures in the Scriptures. God is not bound to his own best (or even canonical) witnesses in all details, and this is most evident in regard to the figure of the Messiah. Many people, not just John, found Jesus to be an enigma. Many do today. Old ties need to be broken in order to see new connections.

The question of 11:3 is perennial: Is Jesus the one to come—the one who brings salvation—or shall we look for another? Each person will have to answer the question for himself or herself, but not necessarily alone. Within the community of faith, faith is given birth and nurtured in the individual. Faith arises in the heart and life of a person who sees that in spite of all in our world that would have us say no, the biblical story culminating in Jesus as the Christ expresses the deepest and most fundamental reality there is. Beyond all signals to the contrary, God lives and embraces fallen humanity in love through Jesus Christ. The ministry of Jesus among men and women is the visible ministry of the invisible God. We need not try to prove that Jesus is the Messiah, as though that were even possible. We need rather to tell the story and witness to him as his body in the world.

The Fourth Sunday in Advent

Lutheran	Roman Catholic	Episcopal	Common Lectionary
Isa. 7:10–14	Isa. 7:10–14	Isa. 7:10–17	Isa. 7:10–16
Rom. 1:1–7	Rom. 1:1–7	Rom. 1:1–7	Rom. 1:1–7
Matt. 1:18–25	Matt. 1:18–24	Matt. 1:18–25	Matt. 1:18–25

EXEGESIS

FIRST LESSON: ISAIAH 7:10–16. The passage relates an encounter between the prophet Isaiah of Jerusalem and Ahaz, king of Judah. More precisely, as 7:1 indicates, the encounter took place at the time of the Syro-Ephraimite war (734–733 B.C.), when the kings of Syria and Ephraim (Israel)—by name, Rezin and Pekah—sought to overthrow Ahaz and replace him with a puppet king (7:6) who would join their coalition against Assyria. Eventually the response of Ahaz would be to appeal to Tiglath-pileser of Assyria for help (cf. 2 Kings 16:5–9).

In 7:10–13 there is an interchange between Isaiah and Ahaz. The Lord speaks through the prophet, inviting Ahaz to seek a "sign" from God of any kind imaginable. Ahaz responds with pious words, "I will not put the Lord to a test," which are probably intended to cloak his real intent, that is, to refuse to listen to the prophet. Isaiah's response is rather sarcastic: Ahaz's refusal to listen only makes God weary with him.

Isaiah goes on to articulate his famous line, saying that the Lord will nevertheless give a sign to Ahaz: "Behold, a young woman shall conceive and bear a son, and shall call his name Immanuel" (7:14). In the Hebrew text the subject of the sentence is *'almah* ("young woman," not necessarily a virgin), preceded by the definite article, so, "the young woman," a woman of marriageable age. In the Septuagint, which is quoted at Matt. 1:23, the definite article has been retained, but the noun has been translated by *parthenos* (virgin), hence, "the virgin." Following the Hebrew text, it is clear that Isaiah has a specific person in mind—not a virgin, but a young married woman—and commentators have suggested (without unanimity) that she would have been either one of the king's wives (or consorts), the wife of Isaiah himself, or another woman known to both Isaiah and Ahaz. Further, the verb concerning conception is in the perfect tense: she *"has* conceived and will bear a son," so she is pregnant at the time of the prophet's address to the king. In the Septuagint (followed in Matt. 1:23), both verbs are in future tense. Once this child is born, the mother "shall call his name Immanuel," meaning "God with us." (The LXX has "you [the king] shall call his name . . .''; and Matt. 1:23 has "they shall call his name. . . .") It is at this point—when the child is named—that the sign will have been given to Ahaz. The naming of the child will signify that the Syro-Ephraimite threat to Judah is over.

In the following verses (10:15–16), the assurance to Ahaz is sustained. As soon as the child can eat solid food, he will have moral discernment (10:15), but even prior to that time, both Syria and Israel will be deserted (10:16), that is, Assyria will overtake them, so they will not be a threat at all. This came to pass in 722 B.C.

SECOND LESSON: ROMANS 1:1–7. The passage constitutes the formal opening of the Letter to the Romans, in which customary forms of Greco-Roman letters can be seen. First, there is the A to B (sender to addressee) pattern: "Paul . . . to all God's beloved in Rome" (1:1, 7). Second, there is the greeting. In ordinary Greek letters this consists of a single verb, *chairein* ("greetings"), but in Paul's letters this is replaced by his use of the noun *charis* ("grace"), which is somewhat like the verb in sound. To this he adds the usual Jewish greeting, "peace" (*shalom* in Hebrew; *eirēnē* in Greek). These (grace and peace) are from God and from Christ, says Paul. He is able to convey them from God and Christ on the grounds that he is an apostle or emissary of the risen Christ.

The section is rather long for an epistolary opening. This is due in large part to the fact that the church at Rome had not been founded by Paul. He wrote the letter—apparently during his three-month stay at Corinth (cf. Rom. 15:25–27 with Acts 19:21; 20:3; 1 Cor. 16:3–5), which would have been about A.D. 55—in anticipation of his visit to Rome on his way to Spain (Rom. 1:10–13; 15:24, 28). In preparing for this visit, Paul makes some points about himself and his gospel. In saying that he is a servant of Christ (1:1), he identifies himself with other Christians, whom he calls servants (6:22; 1 Cor. 7:22; 2 Cor. 4:5). But in speaking of himself as an apostle (1:1) and of his apostleship (1:5) he distinguishes himself as one "called" and "set apart" (1:1) for a particular purpose, the proclamation of the gospel. In discussing terminological designations of various persons, it should be noted that Paul speaks of the Roman addressees as (1) persons "called of Jesus Christ" (1:6), (2) "God's beloved" (1:7), and (3) "saints" (1:7). They are therefore not regarded by Paul as a potential pool to increase his own mission field (1:12 and 15:20 speak explicitly against that). Yet, at the same time, he has no question about speaking to these people with the authority of an apostle.

Of major exegetical interest is the material in 1:3–4. Although not unanimous in this judgment, major interpreters consider the material (beginning with "who" in 1:3) to have been derived from a pre-Pauline creed (which would have begun with a reference to Jesus prior to "who"), which Paul inserts here. Although less certain, it may be that the creed was known to the church at Rome, and so Paul's use of it would signal his acceptance of it as a statement of faith, and at the same time he would strike a rapport with his readers. It speaks clearly of Jesus as being "of the seed of David according to the flesh," but one can hardly translate the next clause without making exegetical judgments. The RSV translation is fitting, and it can hardly be improved. In our judgment, a primitive adoptionism is implied here, that is, according to this early creed, Jesus the descendant of David was designated God's Son for the first time at his resurrection (Easter). That was his moment of coronation as Son of God/Messiah. Paul himself, of course, is not adoptionistic in his thinking, for he affirms the preexistence of Christ (Rom. 8:3; 2 Cor. 8:9; Gal. 4:4), and even in the context of Romans the sharp adoptionistic edge of this creed is rounded off somewhat by Paul's introductory clause in 1:3a. For Paul, the creedal statement is about God's Son, and Easter would have been the occasion on which he was certified ("designated," RSV) to be the one he had been from eternity.

Paul writes that it is through the risen Lord that he has received his apostleship (cf. Gal. 1:11–17). The purpose of his apostleship was to bring about "obedience of faith," which is a phrase subject to different interpretations, but could mean simply faith that consists of obedience (hence, a genitive of apposition). Moreover, it is an apostleship to be carried on among "all the nations." Paul is conventionally called the "apostle to the gentiles" (11:13; cf. 15:9; Gal. 1:16; 2:9); the Greek word *ethnē* can be translated as either "gentiles" or "nations." At Rom. 1:5 the RSV has "nations," which seems to be required by the use of "all" (so "all the nations"). The phrase is important. As Paul projects his mission to Rome and on to Spain (and who knows where beyond that?), he thinks in terms of the various "nations" of his day to be reached with the gospel. Among these "nations" can be found the Roman Christians (1:6), who are among those called by the gospel, loved by God, and enrolled among the saints.

GOSPEL: MATTHEW 1:18–25.   The Gospel of Matthew has no Nativity story per se. The opening verse of the present passage seems to promise one, but it is followed by details prior to the Nativity. And after the passage has been read, we go on to find ourselves in the story of the visit of the Magi (2:1–12). The Nativity itself has been missed.

Matthew and Luke, for all their similarities concerning the origins of Jesus (names of his parents, his birth in Bethlehem, the virginal conception, and his Davidic descent), have major differences in detail. The account of Joseph's deliberation of possible divorce is peculiar to Matthew alone.

According to the evangelist, this deliberation took place after Mary "had been betrothed to Joseph" (1:18). The marriage custom of the day involved two stages. First came the betrothal, a marriage contract that can be broken only by divorce (cf. 1:19). This was followed by a second step (often with a marriage feast) in which the groom took his wife to his home. The verb *paralambanō* (RSV, "to take") in 1:20 and 1:24 actually has the meaning "to take home" one's wife, thus referring to the second step.

Joseph's reaction to knowledge of Mary's pregnancy is to suspect her of adultery. Although the law would allow for her death by stoning (Deut. 22:20–21), Joseph "resolved to divorce her quietly." But an angel intervenes, telling him in a dream not to refrain from going through with the second step of the marriage custom. The angel also tells him how it is that she is pregnant and announces Jesus' forthcoming birth. As the story unfolds, it appears that Mary knows nothing of Joseph's deliberations or his encounter with the angel in a dream.

The next few lines are filled with christological significance. Joseph is to name the child "Jesus," as it is known in English (based on the Greek *Iēsous*). The Greek name is derived from the Hebrew *Yehoshuah* (Joshua in English), which means "Yahweh is salvation" (or perhaps "Yahweh will save"). The child born to Mary is to be given that name as a designation of his function, which is to save his people from their sins (1:21). The way that is envisioned by Matthew is that Jesus not only grants forgiveness of sins in his earthly ministry (9:2) but does so also in his postresurrection reign—where he has all authority (28:18), and from where he exercises that authority through the ministry of the forgiveness of sins by his disciples in the church (16:19; 18:19; 26:28; cf. 9:8).

In 1:22–23 Matthew provides the first of his frequent "formula quotations" in which he declares that an event has taken place to fulfill what a prophet has spoken, followed by a quotation (others are found at 2:15, 17–18, 23; 4:14; 8:17; 12:17; 13:14, 35; 21:4; 27:9). The quotation of Isa. 7:14 is based on a Greek version of the Old Testament, in which the term *parthenos* ("virgin") is used. The wording is exactly like that of the LXX except that in 1:23b Matthew has "they shall call," while the LXX has "you shall call." (On the historical background of Isa. 7:14, see the Exegesis for the First Lesson.) The evangelist sees the coming of God's Son into the world as the fulfillment of the promise given through Isaiah. The birth of Jesus is the sign of God's presence, "God with us." Matthew's Christology is rich and varied. Although he does not apply to Jesus the title "God" (as at John 20:28 or Titus 2:13), the coming of Jesus implies the advent of God's favor and presence among his people.

The last two verses (1:24–25) focus on Joseph. He takes Mary into his home as his wife, and then, after the child is born, names him Jesus in obedience to the command. Verse 1:25a functions to emphasize the virginal conception by the Spirit.

HOMILETICAL INTERPRETATION

FIRST LESSON: ISAIAH 7:10–16. Clearly, the reason this text is read at worship on a Sunday in Advent is that, according to tradition, it foretells the birth of the Messiah of a virgin mother. It would be natural for a sermon based upon it to relate it to the Gospel for the Day—it is hardly possible not to. So close to Christmas, it would also be unwise not to do so.

Yet even though a relationship cannot and should not be avoided, it is possible to design a sermon that keeps the Old Testament setting and proclamation in view. We have a story of God's promise of his abiding presence and salvation in spite of human obstinacy. King Ahaz wants nothing in the way of divine help ("I will not ask," 7:12). But the promise of the Immanuel sign and of subsequent deliverance from the threat of the kings of Syria and Ephraim (Israel) is given to him in spite of his stubborn attitude and behavior. Isaiah communicates the divine promise even in a seemingly hopeless situation. Although a word of judgment seems fitting for the king, there is a word of grace.

The story illustrates a familiar dynamic of the divine-human relationship. For whatever reasons (pride, lack of faith, lethargy, hostility, etc.), humanity as a whole and individuals in particular are unwilling to call upon, honor, and serve God. And it is that unwillingness and inaction that wearies God! That dynamic is illustrated in 7:12–13. But fortunately the relationship does not rest upon human initiative. God establishes a relationship with us by means of God's own actions. That is apparent in the case of Ahaz. It is abundantly clear in the sending of God's Son Jesus Christ as the sign of God's presence among us, which signifies the coming salvation of God's people from their sins (Matt. 1:21). Paul expresses the divine initiative well when he writes: "While we were still weak, at the right time Christ died for the ungodly" (Rom. 5:6). He does not say that the Christ event was for the strong, the ready, or the godly.

The Season of Advent can be a time of austerity and judgment. But it should also be a time to hear the gospel of God's encounter with human obstinacy and victory over it. That theme is heard particularly in the Advent hymn, "O come, O come Emmanuel," for its lines speak of the human condition in terms of bondage, but they also celebrate God's coming salvation. God draws near to us, to all his children, so that all of life is pervaded with his presence. But "God is with us" (Immanuel) particularly in Jesus Christ.

SECOND LESSON: ROMANS 1:1–7. The passage is of interest for the Advent Season primarily because (1) it sets forth the claim that the gospel concerning God's Son was promised beforehand by the Old Testament prophets and (2) it links Jesus to the Davidic line (as in the Gospel, Matt. 1:20). Coming as it does at the end of the Advent Season and at the threshold of Christmas, this text provides a bridge between seasons (as does the Gospel for the Day), since it speaks forthrightly of the gospel, which declares that the promises have been fulfilled. Yet one could focus on the two items mentioned above: the prophetic and Davidic (or royal) anticipations of the coming of Christ.

Prophetic anticipations of the "gospel of God" (1:1) have been read each Sunday of the season. All of them anticipate the good news of God's saving work, and the preacher could summarize some of the contents of that expected work. In general, they anticipate a messianic age more than a Messiah per se. Yet it is through Jesus' life, death, and resurrection that we see the fulfillment of these expectations. We see divine power of transformation at work in Jesus' earthly ministry of healing and forgiving sins and in his resurrection and reign over the cosmos. We expect the transformation of all things with his Parousia.

The one promised to come is also the Son of David. We have seen the importance of this concept in our Old Testament lessons as well (esp. Isa. 11:1–10). The expected Messiah would be a descendant of David, to whom the promise had been given that his royal house would endure forever (2 Sam. 7:16; Ps. 89:3–4). The coming of Jesus fulfills this expectation, but with a surprising twist. The one to come was expected to be a royal figure in every way imaginable; surely he was to be as great or greater than David had been. But the royal Son of David is born in humble circumstances; he is rejected by his own people; and it is only by virtue of his resurrection that we know him to be the royal figure he truly is.

A sermon based on Rom. 1:1–7 could thus recapitulate much of the Old Testament material presented during the season (and more besides), showing how the expectations of Israel were both fulfilled in Jesus and more than fulfilled. God had more in store for his people than even his inspired witnesses in ancient Israel could anticipate. We anticipate the Messiah's coming in glory at the end of time. But we know him to be the one who came among us in lowliness and for our salvation long ago. We hear of his birth in the Gospel for the Day. And we celebrate his Nativity the next time we gather together.

GOSPEL: MATTHEW 1:18–25. The text is assigned for the Sunday prior to the Nativity of Our Lord, and except for the very last verse it anticipates that. Yet it is difficult not to read the text as a Nativity account. There must be some way to keep the anticipatory mood of Advent going.

One way to do that would be to focus on the Emmanuel theme connecting the First Lesson and the Gospel for the Day. Matthew picks up on the Emmanuel theme from Isaiah in connection with the promise of the angel to Joseph (1:20–23). The coming of Jesus will signify that "God is with us" for a saving purpose. Of course, that promise has already been fulfilled, for Jesus' birth happened long ago. But we rejoice in Advent for the promise given. That it has been fulfilled does not diminish it; in fact, it makes it even more precious.

The promise of Emmanuel ("God with us") gives meaning to life. We do not see that God is clearly with us in nature or history. True, there are "signals of transcendence" that intimate the presence of God. They are those "phenomena that are to be found within the domain of our 'natural' reality but that appear to point beyond that reality" (Peter L. Berger, *A Rumor of Angels* [Garden City, N.Y.: Doubleday & Co., 1969], 65–66). One can think of phenomena in ordinary life—such as the look across the breakfast table of one's child being enthralled by the hummingbird at the window—that induce wonder, awe, and joy in us about the rightness and goodness of things, and do so at such a profound level that we are brought to a fundamentally religious experience. Similarly, Abraham H. Maslow has spoken of "peak-experiences" common to people, which are moments of "pure, positive happiness when all doubts, all fears, all inhibitions, all tensions, all weaknesses [are] left behind" ("Lessons from the Peak-Experiences," *Journal of Humanistic Psychology* 2 [1962]:9). But these "signals of transcendence" and "peak-experiences" are not with us every day, and they are in fact ambiguous. They are at best intimations, not proofs, of the presence of God.

The one clear sign of God's presence is the one given in the biblical story, if we are willing to see it. Isaiah anticipated a sign some eight hundred years before the birth of Christ. That sign has been given in the coming of Jesus himself. He is the sign of God's presence, Emmanuel. Apart from him, there are no clear signs.

Late in the Season of Advent, on the threshold of Christmas, we anticipate the celebration of Jesus' birth. We do well to celebrate the birth of Jesus not only for what he was to become, but also for what he was in God's purpose. His birth was a sign of God's presence, the culmination of an old hope.

Advent is also a time to anticipate Jesus' future coming in glory. But it is not simply a time of waiting. It is a time for the church itself to be a sign of God's being in the world. It would be appropriate for every congregation to be called Emmanuel Church, for every congregation is a colony that celebrates the presence of God with us and witnesses to that reality in the world.

The Nativity of Our Lord, Christmas Day

Lutheran	Roman Catholic	Episcopal	Common Lectionary
Isa. 9:2–7	Isa. 9:2–7	Isa. 9:2–4, 6–7	Isa. 9:2–7
Titus 2:11–14	Titus 2:11–14	Titus 2:11–14	Titus 2:11–14
Luke 2:1–20	Luke 2:1–14	Luke 2:1–14	Luke 2:1–20

EXEGESIS

FIRST LESSON: ISAIAH 9:2–7. The passage is an "accession oracle" that celebrates the rise of an ideal, messianic king. Interpreters dispute whether it originated during the time of, and from, Isaiah of Jerusalem (eighth century B.C.) or at a later time, but it anticipates the just and effective rule of a king of David's line (9:7) and the consequent peace and security that will follow his accession. What is anticipated is due, moreover, to an act of God: "The zeal of the Lord of hosts will do this" (9:7).

The oracle begins with a focus on a particular people—those "who walked in darkness" (9:2). It appears that the people of the Northern Kingdom are meant, if 9:1 can be our guide. In any case, "light" has appeared and shined upon the people: the day of salvation has come. The people have grounds for joy, since the reign of the king to come will result in good for them.

In 9:4–5 (beginning with "for") the basis for the people's rejoicing is given. The time of oppression and warfare is over. In 9:4 an oppressive ruler—perhaps the king of Assyria—is declared to be undone. The verb in this verse ("broken") is in past tense, but it anticipates what is to be in light of the divine action begun: the oppressor's yoke, staff, and rod have been "broken as on the day of Midian," an allusion to the decisive battle won by Gideon and his men over the Midianites (Judg. 6:33—7:25). The verb in the next verse is future: the boots and uniforms of warriors "will be burned." So sweeping is the prophet's picture of the coming era that both oppression and warfare will be no more; justice and peace will replace them.

When the author speaks of the birth of a child and the giving of a son at 9:6, it is possible that he has the birth of an actual child (a prince of the royal family) in mind, but it is just as likely that he speaks of the accession (or coronation) of a new king. Such language is used for similar purposes at Ps. 2:7 ("You are my son, today I have begotten you," a line used at the enthronement of a king). In any case, it would be at his accession that four titles are applied to the king which, it is hoped, will characterize the qualities of his reign (the four titles are listed as five in the KJV and Handel's *Messiah;* the RSV is correct in having four by its rendering of "Wonderful Counselor" as one title, not two). The titles "Wonderful Counselor" and "Everlasting Father" stress the king's abilities to govern through guidance and concern for his people. The titles "Mighty God" (or "Divine Warrior," as some commentators suggest for better translation) and "Prince of Peace" stress his roles as protector of the people and initiator and keeper of peace within the realm that he governs. Even though the prophet has spoken of the end of warfare in 9:4–5, he is not able to dispense with the imagery of warfare entirely when speaking of the future king. Yet he envisions not only the greatness and power of the coming king's reign in words that can be set to martial music (which Handel accomplished). He also envisions the perpetuity of peace. The prophet alludes at the same time to the perpetuity of the throne of David (cf. 2 Sam. 7:13–16; Ps. 89:4, 29–36). This peaceful reign of the coming king will be attended by "righteousness" and "justice," which shall be established so sure that they will last "for evermore." And although all this seems too much to hope for, the prophet declares that God in his zeal will accomplish it.

SECOND LESSON: TITUS 2:11–14. The Pastoral Epistles (1 and 2 Timothy, Titus) are widely regarded as deutero-Pauline, that is, they were written in the name of Paul, and to represent Paul, after his death by an anonymous writer of the so-called Pauline School. That view will be assumed here.

Prior to our lesson, the writer has written concerning the qualifications of a bishop (1:5–9), the characteristics of false teachers whom he opposes (1:10–16), and the manner of life expected of men, women, and slaves (2:1–10). The larger section (2:11—3:11) in which our text appears is an exposition of life under grace, the basis for the conduct expected. In 2:11–14 itself the writer speaks of the transforming power of the grace of God. It provides the theological basis for what has gone before it, not for what follows.

In 2:11 the writer says that "God's saving grace" (as the Greek can be translated) "has appeared" *(epephanē,* "has been made manifest") for "all people." Undoubtedly the writer has the whole Christ event in mind—not simply the incarnation, but Christ's ministry, death, and resurrection as well—as also at 2 Tim. 1:9–10. In saying that this saving grace has appeared for "all people," the writer opposes heretical teachers (see 1:10–16) who teach that salvation is available only to those who follow their particular prescriptions ("myths" and "human commandments," 1:14). The writer says that God "desires all people to be saved and to come to the knowledge of the truth" (1 Tim. 2:4; cf. 4:10), and in the Christ event that salvation has been manifested for all. Indeed, Christ has "abolished death and brought life and immortality to light," which is made known to all people through the proclamation of the gospel (2 Tim. 1:10).

In 2:12–13a the consequences of the manifestation of the saving grace of God in Christ are drawn out. This grace has an educating effect for life in the world. The Christian renounces "irreligion" (or "impiety," *asebeia),* which is the fruit of heretical teachings (2 Tim. 2:16), and "worldly passions" (a term found only here in the New Testament). On the contrary, this saving grace educates one to a life characterized by the positive qualities of sobriety, uprightness, and godliness "in the present age." The Pastorals have a remarkably positive attitude toward the creation. Christians do not despise the world but live and serve in it, and it is into this world that God's grace has appeared for salvation. Yet at the same time, Christians await a "blessed hope," the content of which is the Parousia of Christ.

The writer now shifts back to christological matters (2:13b–14). Christians expect "the appearing of the glory . . ." (RSV, which is literal). KJV has "the glorious appearing," which is not a literal translation of the Greek, but it catches the thought well. The one to come is "our great God and Savior Jesus Christ." Rarely do the New Testament writers speak of Jesus as God, and even the writer of the Pastorals makes distinctions between Jesus and God (cf. Titus 1:4; 3:4–6). But what the writer affirms is that at his parousia Christ will bear the divine glory and do the saving work of God. In fact, he has already given himself in his death on the cross "to redeem us from all iniquity" (2:14); he "gave himself as a ransom for all" (1 Tim. 2:6), setting us free from the punishment deserved at the final judgment. Moreover, his purpose was to purify us and claim us as his possession (here are echoes of Ezek. 37:23 on purification, and of Exod. 19:5–6; Deut. 4:20; 7:6; 14:2 on a people as God's possession). And this people is "zealous for good deeds." The Christ event is thus an epiphany of God's saving grace for all people, but it is also instructive for those who have claimed this salvation as their own. Those who claim it are a people claimed—Christ's possession—for godly living in the world, zealous for good works.

GOSPEL: LUKE 2:1–20.   The reading consists of two parts: the birth of Jesus (2:1–7) and the adoration of the child by the shepherds (2:8–20). The first of these begins by locating the birth of Jesus in time and place. Concerning the time, it took place during the reign of Caesar Augustus (Roman emperor, 27 B.C.–A.D. 14). So far there is no problem. What Luke adds to this, however, causes chronological problems. He refers to a census (RSV, "enrollment") that Augustus decreed, and he says that this census took place while Quirinius was governor of Syria. But the governorship of Quirinius did not begin until A.D. 6, and the census referred to would have taken place A.D. 6–7 when Judea was incorporated into the province of Syria for Roman administrative purposes (Josephus, *Ant.* 18.1). Such a chronology does not allow for the birth of Jesus within the reign of Herod (1:5; Matt. 2:1), who died in 4 B.C. The birth of Jesus was probably before Herod's death rather than after the enrollment decree. In any case, Luke refers to this enrollment to provide an explanation for Mary and Joseph's eighty-five-mile journey from Nazareth to Bethlehem—although whether such a trek was required by law is questionable—where both Luke (2:4) and Matthew (2:1) place the birth. Bethlehem was the town from whence the father of David originated (1 Sam. 17:12). While the couple was there, the child was born to Mary, who was betrothed to Joseph (2:5), which means that she was legally his wife (see the Exegesis for Matt. 1:18–25, Advent 4). Jesus was Mary's first-born son (2:7), which implies that she had subsequent sons (cf. the use of the adjective in the Septuagint at Gen. 25:25; 48:18), and these are named in Mark 6:3. Yet it is not impossible (in keeping with Roman Catholic tradition) to take the term as a Semitism and to refer simply to Jesus' having the rights of the first-born (cf. Exod. 13:2, taken up by Luke at 2:23). The birth in Bethlehem is in keeping with the prophecy of the birthplace of Israel's future ruler in Mic. 5:2.

The section devoted to the adoration of the shepherds (2:8–20) contains a series of pictorial scenes. The first is the appearance of an angel of the Lord to the shepherds (2:8–12). Appropriately the angelophany incites fear, but the angel tells the shepherds not to be afraid (cf. 1:13) and announces to them the good news of the birth of one who bears three titles: Savior, Christ, and Lord (2:11). All three titles have a background in Judaism, even in the Old Testament, but to combine them and apply them to one person on one occasion presupposes a post-Easter christological development, which is here retrojected to the time of Jesus' birth. The angelic chorus (2:13–14) rounds off this scene with the singing of the Gloria in Excelsis. The RSV rendering "peace among men with whom he is pleased" is an expansion of the Greek (according to superior texts), which can be translated "peace among persons of favor" (i.e., God's favor). The song ascribes glory to God in heaven and declares peace to humanity on earth; and the latter is based on God's favor.

The visit of the shepherds (2:15–18) takes place in response to the angel's declaration: "You will find a babe wrapped in swaddling cloths and lying in a manger" (2:12). That is exactly what they find (2:16). But what is the "saying" they made known (2:17)? It must be the declaration of the angels that the child is the "Savior, who is Christ the Lord" (2:11). To whom did they make it known? According to 2:19, it seems to be to residents of Bethlehem. These people are left in wonderment, but Mary (who knows the identity of her son; cf. 1:31–33, 35) kept all that was said, pondering everything in her heart (the presumed locale of thought and understanding). The story closes with the return of the shepherds to their work. They glorify God for what they have "heard and seen."

Although the passage does not synchronize well with the actual political history of the era, Luke clearly intends by his grand summary statements concerning secular rulers and their rule to emphasize that, while the birth of the Messiah took place under the normal circumstance of historical life, its happening in Bethlehem (rather than Nazareth) was by divine design; God can rule history even through the decrees of earthly emperors. Only divine guidance of the historical process can account for the entry of Jesus Christ into the world. His birth inaugurates a new stage in the history of salvation.

HOMILETICAL INTERPRETATION

FIRST LESSON: ISAIAH 9:2–7. The birth of a child is universally considered a moment of beginnings—not only of the child's life, but of the world to which the child belongs. A family is rejuvenated, and relationships change. Wherever a monarchy exists (in either ancient or modern places), the birth of a child who is to be heir or heiress is a day of national rebirth.

It is in this universal symbol—the birth of a child—that the connection between the oracle of Isaiah and the coming of Jesus as the Christ into the world can be seen. Isaiah anticipated the rise of the greatest king yet in the history of Israel. His reign will have an impact not only on Israel but upon the whole world. He will be worthy of the titles bestowed upon him (9:6), and the effects of his reign will last forever (9:7). Because of this king, there is a renewal of the people.

The coming of Jesus into the world, as portrayed by the story of his birth in Bethlehem, signifies the world's renewal. No longer are things the same. The titles attributed to the king (9:6) apply to Jesus properly only in consequence of his resurrection (not his birth), and only the risen Lord has an everlasting kingdom. Yet the verses (9:6–7) are in future tense.

What is said of the great king to come applies to the child born in Bethlehem, anticipating his post-Easter reign.

The most striking characteristic of the reign of the king to come is peace on earth. The first lesson anticipates peace, and the Gospel (Luke 2:14) declares it. The basis for the difference is that the first looks for peace among people, and the last speaks of peace between God and humanity. We should not trivialize the former (a task to be about) by sentimentalizing the latter (a gift given). The Prince of Peace of whom Isaiah speaks is one who comes to change the world.

SECOND LESSON: TITUS 2:11–14. "For the grace of God has appeared for the salvation of all people" (2:11). This grace has appeared in the coming of Jesus into the world.

Two aspects of this verse can be developed homiletically. The first is the act, the Christ event. The God of the Scriptures is a God of action, and God's acts can be recounted: the creation of the world, the election of Abraham, the exodus from Egypt, the making of the Sinai covenant, the sending of the prophets, and finally the sending of God's Son. All of these are manifestations of God's grace. The last of them, the sending of God's Son, therefore culminates a series of manifestations of grace; it is not the only or the first act of God.

There is something decisive and particular about the act of God in sending the Son, for it was "for the salvation of all people" (2:11). And if Christ came for the sake of all, all must be given the opportunity to hear the good news.

The second aspect that could be developed is the way the verse speaks of Christ. The writer clearly speaks of him and his incarnation when he says that "the grace of God has appeared." Why does he not simply say that "the Son of God has appeared"? The writer should say what he means! Yet there is something tantalizing in the way he puts it. The appearance of Jesus in our world manifests, or reveals, the way things are with God, the ground of all being. At the basis of all things there is a power of reconciling love, the God of Israel and the whole world, who is revealed in the Scriptures and, above all, in Jesus.

This means that Christmas is not first of all about Mary and Joseph and the child Jesus. It is a story about God and God's doings in the world. Christmas can have a fairy-tale character, thanks to carols, cards, commerce, and yes, even to congregations. But it need not, and it should not. Its message is for sojourners in the real world. Christmas has to do with foundations on which to build one's life, things one can rely on. It has to do with the good news that the appearance of Jesus in history was the appearance of the good will and grace of the Lord of the cosmos.

GOSPEL: LUKE 2:1–20.   Christmas is a time for thinking of things new and old, small and great. The new is the birth of the Savior; the old is our knowing that this birth took place centuries ago, and that it has been celebrated by countless forebears and even ourselves down to the present day.

But it is with things small and great that God deals at Christmas. We see this in our text. There are the great figures of history—Caesar Augustus, Quirinius the governor of Syria, and King Herod. There is the multitude of angels, and there is also the royal family of ancient Israel, the house and lineage of David.

But there are also things small that belong to the story. These include the young couple Mary and Joseph, who are in a critical situation: Mary is far along in her pregnancy, and yet they have to get to Bethlehem, because Caesar has given orders. There are the shepherds, poor men, who were filled with fear at the appearance of the host of angels. And there is the smallest one of all, Jesus, the newborn child.

The dynamics of small and great can be felt in our own lives. There is the old saying that "Christmas is for children." And so it is. But it is not for them only. God deals with both great and small, adult and child. Surely one can observe Christmas as an adult and in an adult way. A clue to how this could be possible comes from Dag Hammarskjöld's reflections on Christmas eve in 1957:

> In Thy wind—in Thy light—
> How insignificant is everything else, how small are we
> —and how happy in that which alone is great.
> *(Markings* [New York: Alfred A. Knopf, 1964], 161)

The splendor of Christmas, the grandeur of God's gift, Jesus' entry into the world—these are great indeed, and in their presence we are so small. We need not pretend that we are small children. We need only hear the story of Christmas in the hush of solemn worship. In God's light, and in the presence of his love and power, we are so small. We are God's children.

The First Sunday after Christmas

Lutheran	Roman Catholic	Episcopal	Common Lectionary
Isa. 63:7–9	Sir. 3:2–6, 12–14	Isa. 61:10—62:3	Isa. 63:7–9
Gal. 4:4–7	Col. 3:12–21	Gal. 3:23–25, 4:4–7	Heb. 2:10–18
Matt. 2:13–15, 19–23	Matt. 2:13–15, 19–23	John 1:1–18	Matt. 2:13–15, 19–23

EXEGESIS

FIRST LESSON: ISAIAH 63:7–9. The passage is from Trito-Isaiah (Isaiah 56–66), which is customarily assigned to the postexilic era (after 539 B.C.). Further, it is located within a unit (63:7—64:11) that has been classified form critically as a psalm of lament, specifically, a community lament. Nevertheless, the lament proper is not expressed until 63:15. All of 63:7–14 (which includes our text) is a historical prologue prior to the address to God (63:15–16) and the author's complaint against God (63:17–19).

In the opening verse (63:7) the author announces that he will call to mind the gracious acts of the Lord. The two terms that the RSV translates as "steadfast love" and "praises" are actually both plural nouns in the Hebrew text and can mean, respectively, God's "acts of love" (plural for *hesed)* and his "praiseworthy deeds." The lines alert us to the author's listing of the deeds of God which follows. His recounting of such deeds involves a process of calling them forth into the present for edifying effect.

In the next two verses (63:8–9) the recounting takes place. First, God has called Israel "my people," an act of election. This people will live in fidelity to God; they "will not deal falsely." While the indicative mood is naturally used concerning Israel's election, it is less natural that it should be used in the clause regarding Israel's obligation (not to deal falsely). It expresses divine confidence in Israel. But of course it expects too much! The charge will come soon enough in the lament (64:5–7) that Israel has gone astray. In fact, even the statement of Israel's election is met with the "as if not" of 63:19: "We have become"—in a later time—"like those over whom thou hast never ruled, like those who are not called by thy name." Nevertheless, the psalm expresses confidence in God's gracious election and care. Indeed, God is Israel's "Savior," Israel's protector and deliverer from consequent troubles.

The last verse (63:9) presents text-critical and translation problems. Various interpreters maintain that the RSV rendering is inadequate. The NEB reflects a more critical (and superior) base: "It was no envoy, no angel, but he himself that delivered them." (If this is correct, the "angel" of the RSV has to go, and one of the major connections to our Gospel for the Day—where an angel plays a role in the rescue of Jesus, Matt. 2:13, 19—is severed.) In any case, the verse recalls events associated with the exodus from Egypt. The expressions concerning God's love and pity for God's people recall Exod. 3:7 where the Lord says, "I have seen the affliction of my people . . . I know their sufferings." The redemption spoken of recalls the exodus event itself (Exodus 13–15), and the image of God's carrying the people, as a parent carries a child, sums up the whole matter: God has preserved and delivered the people purely out of love and pity. For other passages using the imagery of God's carrying the people, see Exod. 19:4; Deut. 1:31 ("The Lord your God bore you, as a man bears his son"); and Isa. 46:4. On the divine motivation for God's saving work, see Deut. 7:7–8: "It was not because you were more in number than any other people that the Lord set his love upon you and chose you . . . but it is because the Lord loves you."

SECOND LESSON: GALATIANS 4:4–7 or HEBREWS 2:10–18. The lectionary readings vary widely. We shall comment on the two that appear in the Lutheran/Episcopal and Common lectionaries.

Paul's Letter to the Galatians was written to congregations (plural; see 1:2) he had founded in Asia Minor, and which had subsequently been affected by persons (usually thought to be infiltrators from outside, but this is not certain) proclaiming a "different gospel" (1:6, 9), which is not really a gospel at all (1:7). Our passage comes from the central core of the letter (3:1—5:12) in which Paul does battle with the views of those who proclaim the alternate message as he scolds his readers and exhorts them to return to the gospel he preaches. According to the letter itself, these persons have persuaded Paul's converts to "desire to be under the law" (4:21), as though it is by "works of the law" of Moses that one can gain justification before God (3:11, 18). They promote circumcision (5:2–3, 12), the observance of set days and seasons (4:10), and the worship of the "elements of the universe" (4:3, 8–11).

The passage assigned in the lectionary follows shortly after a section in which Paul discusses the function of the law in human history (3:19–25). He claims here that the law's place in the past was that of a "custodian" (3:24) until the coming of Christ. But with the coming of Christ, he says, Christians are no longer "under" the law; they are "in" Christ by means of faith (3:26). The thinking expressed here comes to expression also in Romans, where Paul says that "Christ is the end of the law for justification to everyone who believes" (10:4), and that Christians "are not under law but under grace" (6:14).

In the first verse of our passage (4:4) Paul speaks of the timing of the incarnation; it was "when the fullness of time *(plērōma tou chronou)* had come." The concept is not that of the world's readiness, as is often suggested (e.g., that there was a common language). What Paul speaks of, rather, is time's fulfillment, an eschatological event, in which God's saving work has come into history, inaugurating a new age. God's "sending" of his Son (an expression found also in Rom. 8:3) was for a redemptive purpose, which is stated in two purpose clauses: "In order that *(hina)* he might redeem those under the law, in order that *(hina)* we might receive adoption" (4:5). The first of these clauses speaks of the redemption of Jews; the second must refer to all Christians who receive adoption as children of God through baptism. But the primary interest in this passage during the Christmas Season will be the Christology of 4:4. The preexistent Son, says Paul, was sent by God into the world by means of incarnation. The phrase "born of woman" affirms the true humanity of Jesus. It does not presuppose knowledge of a virginal conception; a similar expression is used, for example, at Matt. 11:11 ("among those born of women there has risen no one greater than John the Baptist"). There is no hint of Paul's knowledge of the virginal conception in any of his writings. The concept of virginal conception precludes preexistence and incarnation. Since it makes the "genesis" (Matt. 1:18) or advent of the Son dependent on conception by the Holy Spirit nine months prior to his nativity, the concept of virginal conception has no place for the preexistence of the Son from eternity. But Paul rather routinely affirms preexistence and incarnation (1 Cor. 8:6; 2 Cor. 8:9; Phil. 2:5–7). Further, he says that the Son was "born under the law," which affirms the Jewish origins of Jesus, whom Paul knows to be the offspring of Abraham (3:16) and a descendant of David (Rom. 1:3). In sum, the Christology expressed here is that the eternal Son of God became enfleshed in Jesus of Nazareth, a truly human being of the people Israel.

In 4:6–7 Paul speaks of the consequences of the redemptive work of God in Christ. The redemptive work itself is not spelled out. But Paul has already referred to it at 3:13 where he says that Christ, being crucified, bore the divine curse that is upon one who is hanged (Deut. 21:23). This concept can be worked out further in reference to Rom. 8:3: God's condemnation of sin (the sin of all humanity) was exercised at the cross. The result is that humanity is set free from the divine condemnation. Believers (Christians) are "adopted" already through baptism to become children of God. To such persons God has sent forth *(exapesteilen,* 4:6; the same verb is used in 4:4) "the Spirit of his Son." The phrase is not used elsewhere, but like "Spirit of Christ" (Rom. 8:9; Phil. 1:19) and "Spirit of the Lord" (2 Cor. 3:17), it refers to the Holy Spirit. The Spirit enters into the human heart (cf. Rom. 5:5) and prompts the children of God to speak of God as "Abba, Father." The term "Abba" (used also at Rom. 8:15) is the Aramaic word used within the family to call upon one's father, and so it is a term of intimacy. It must have been taken over by Greek-speaking Christians from the Aramaic-speaking Palestinian church. The use of "Abba" indicates a sense of intimacy with God from earliest Christianity, and its use is most likely characteristic of Jesus' own speech about God. The final verse (4:7) is a conclusion to the whole argument of 3:1—4:6. By God's redemptive work in Christ, humanity has been redeemed; believers are children of God (the terms "son" and "sons" of the passage can be expressed in inclusive language, as at 4:3) and inheritors of the promise given to Abraham (3:18) that in him all the nations will be blessed (3:8), which is confirmed in Christ (3:16).

The passage assigned from Hebrews (2:10–18), like Gal. 4:4–7, is incarnational, stressing the humanity of Christ. He is called here by the title "pioneer" *(archēgos)*, the one who leads his people to their final destiny (eternal salvation; cf. 12:2). He and his people have "all one origin" alike (2:11), which is God, and he considers human beings his brothers and sisters. The quotations from the Old Testament (2:12–13) are from Ps. 22:22 and Isa. 8:17–18. They are presented by the author of Hebrews as words spoken by the preexistent Christ as proofs of his common origin with men and women. By partaking of flesh and blood (2:14) he was "made lower than the angels" for his earthly career (2:9). There he had a redemptive work to perform, which he did by rendering the devil powerless (rather than to "destroy" him as in RSV). That happened when he passed through death and entered directly into the heavenly sanctuary (9:24; cf. 4:14; 8:1–2), escaping the devil, and at the same time opening up a "new and living way" for his people to enter into the heavenly sanctuary as well (10:19–20). Death is now but a threshold into the heavenly sanctuary. The author resumes his incarnational emphasis by saying that Christ was like the rest of humanity in every respect, even undergoing suffering and temptation (but at 4:15 the writer adds that he was without sin). He was and is therefore sympathetic to the human condition. He does two things on our behalf: he makes expiation for sins, and he helps those who are tempted. He is involved in both redemptive and sanctifying works. But these are possible only because of his incarnation.

GOSPEL: MATTHEW 2:13–15, 19–23.   The passage narrates the flight of the holy family from Judea to Egypt, their return, and their move to Nazareth of Galilee. The massacre of the innocents (2:16–18) is omitted.

Matthew's account of details surrounding the Nativity agrees with Luke's in placing the birth of Jesus in Bethlehem of Judea (Matt. 2:1; Luke 2:4–

7, 15). But it differs in that Luke portrays Mary and Joseph as residents of Nazareth in Galilee (2:4), and Matthew seems to take for granted that they are residents of Bethlehem, so that Jesus is born at the home of his parents, and that is where the Magi come to adore him (2:11). It is only after the return from the sojourn in Egypt that Joseph "withdrew to the district of Galilee" and "went and dwelt" in the city called Nazareth. The move was due to a warning not to remain in "the land of Israel" (2:22), which is assumed to be the homeland, and that the Scriptures might be fulfilled (2:23).

It is striking that in this account Joseph has dreams no less than three times (2:13, 19, 22), and in each case he receives instructions. The association between Joseph and dreams (see also 1:20; 2:12) recalls the Joseph of the Old Testament, who also had dreams (Gen. 37:5–10; 42:9) and interpreted the dreams of others (40:9–19; 41:1–36). There too the dreams are considered to be media of revelation (41:25). There are additional likenesses to suggest that Matthew's account in 2:13–23 is based on Old Testament material: (1) in the Old Testament Joseph is responsible for bringing the Hebrew people into Egypt (Gen. 42:1—47:28); in Matthew's Gospel Joseph brings the holy family there (2:13–14); (2) Pharaoh sought to exterminate the male infants of Israel (Exod. 1:15–22), and Herod sought to kill all the male babies in the region of Bethlehem (Matt. 2:16–18); (3) but Moses escaped death (Exod. 2:1–10), and so does Jesus (Matt. 2:14); (4) Israel is called out of Egypt and delivered through the exodus (Exod. 13:7—14:31; Hos. 11:1), and so Joseph brings Jesus and his mother out of Egypt (Matt. 2:15, 20–21). The parallels lead to the conclusion that much of what Matthew relates in chapters 1 and 2 is therefore midrashic. The central drama of Israel's redemption is recapitulated in the story of the infant Jesus. The stage is set for the constitution of a redeemed people into a body, the church of Jesus Christ. (The Old Testament parallel would be the constitution of Israel as a covenant people at Sinai.)

The assigned reading locates the flight to Egypt before the death of Herod (2:13), which was in 4 B.C. The return to Israel and the move to Nazareth are after Herod's death (2:19). Herod was succeeded by his son Archelaus in Judea (4 B.C.–A.D. 6; he also ruled Samaria and Idumea), as Matt. 2:22 has it. Other parts of the kingdom fell to Herod Antipas (Galilee and Perea, 4 B.C.–A.D. 39) and Philip (northern Transjordan, 4 B.C.–A.D. 34). Archelaus, as it turned out, was a brutal and insensitive ruler, and Augustus banished him to Gaul in A.D. 6. In any case, the family settled in Nazareth of Galilee. This, for Matthew, was to fulfill prophecy (2:23). Although the verse is cast in the usual form of a Matthean "formula quotation" (see discussion of the form in the Exegesis of Matt. 1:18–25), there is actually no Old Testament text that reads like the supposed quotation. Various attempts have been made to explain its origins. The most common explanation is that the supposed quotation is actually an allusion to Isa. 11:1, "There shall come forth a shoot from the stump of Jesse, and a branch [neṣer in Hebrew] shall grow out of his roots." According to this view, the term neṣer was a messianic designation (as in the Aramaic Targum and some rabbinic sources). In any case, the function of the verse is an apologetic one, and that is to show why the Messiah could come from Nazareth—for Jesus was commonly known as "Jesus of Nazareth" (Matt. 26:71; John 1:45)—when the prophet had declared that he would come from Bethlehem (Mic. 5:2, which is quoted already in Matt. 2:6).

HOMILETICAL INTERPRETATION

FIRST LESSON: ISAIAH 63:7–9. This passage has special associations with Christmas in two ways—God's activities and God's relationship to us. First, God is called "Savior" in our passage (63:8). At Christmas we sing, "Christ the Savior is born." But the word "Savior" had been used already in Old Testament times in speaking about God. The God of the Old Testament is not only the Creator but the Savior as well. He is known as Savior especially in connection with the exodus from Egypt (cf. Ps. 106:21; Hos. 13:4), but not only there. The prophet Jeremiah confesses that the people of his day are sinful, frequently backsliding, but calls God their Savior and the hope of Israel (14:7–9). And Deutero-Isaiah says that Israel has no Savior but God alone (43:3, 11; 45:15, 21; 49:26).

Christmas therefore does not mark the beginning of the story of redemption. God is Savior already in Old Testament times. In the Season of Christmas we do celebrate something decisive, however. That is the birth of the Savior among us in Jesus Christ. Jesus is the incarnation (enfleshment) of the Savior known already in the story and praises of Israel. God has sent forth the Son as the embodiment and expression of who God is and what God does. God is the redeeming God.

The second association this passage has with Christmas is its imagery of God's carrying his people as a parent carries a child. During the Season of Christmas, as this lesson is read, we think of the parents of Jesus carrying their child. But long before that, God cared for Israel, and the prophet found the imagery of a parent carrying a child the most fitting analogy for the relationship. One can picture here a young child riding on its mother's hip or on its father's shoulders. The child looks out on the world with confidence from the position of lofty observation and safety. So the people of Israel, says the prophet, have been led and protected by God in times and places both good and bad.

Within the glow of the Christmas Season, when the picture of the holy family is center stage, we should let that particular picture speak of a more universal reality: our relationship with God, and God's to us, is analogous to that between a parent and a young child. God cares for us in all circumstances. That understanding goes back in time to the Old Testament era. God's sending forth the Son for our redemption confirms it.

SECOND LESSON: GALATIANS 4:4–7 or HEBREWS 2:10–18. The passage from Galatians reflects a lyrical quality that is fitting for the Christmas Season. It speaks of time, incarnation, adoption, and the divine–human relationship. A sermon might touch on all of these themes.

The coming and going of holidays, seasons, and years remind us of the passing of time. Seeing friends and relatives after long intervals, and seeing the changes in them that the aging process brings, makes us aware of time's passing. And thoughts of time can engender thoughts of the meaning of time and its relationship to the larger scheme of things. Plato knew this a long time ago when he called time "a moving image of eternity" and said that time even "intimates eternity" *(Timaeus* 37d, 38a). It seems that time and eternity run on parallel tracks, time being subject to eternity.

But there are moments within time when the eternal is present in force. The temporal moment infused by eternity is more than an ordinary moment. It has a "surplus of meaning." And that is what the apostle Paul points to when he speaks of God's sending the Son in the "fullness of time." As Emil Brunner has put it, "The historical process which is based in the will of God, has now reached the point where God can create that through which He wills to reveal the meaning of all history" *(The Christian Doctrine of Creation and Redemption* [Philadelphia: Westminster Press, 1952], 237). God's sending the Son into the world was a moment of revelation and redemption. It was a moment of revelation because it disclosed the nature and purpose of God and the meaning of history—that all things are moving toward their redemption (cf. Rom. 8:18–25). But it was also a moment of redemption because it was the means by which God dealt with sin (see Exegesis) and set us free for fellowship with God and with humanity in all its variety.

The Nativity, so recently celebrated, displays the picture of the birth of a child, Jesus. This Jesus was the Son of God in a particular way. He represented God and had a relationship to God that surpassed every other divine–human relationship. Yet, because the Son of God has redeemed us, we have been set into a relationship with God that overcomes all that separates us from God. We can call upon God as a child calls upon his or her father. Luther put matters well in his *Small Catechism* when he wrote concerning the first line of the Lord's Prayer ("Our Father in heaven"): "Here God encourages us to believe that he is truly our Father and we are his children. We therefore are to pray to him with complete confidence just as children speak to their loving father." Although there are objections from time to time to speaking of God as Father (either because some people have had bad relationships with their fathers, or because of concerns for inclusivity), only an extreme iconoclasm insists on eliminating the imagery. Our imagery about God should be expanded, not reduced. What Paul expresses in Aramaic and Greek (Abba, *patēr*) is intended as good news, and the imagery goes back to the very earliest community of Christians, and even to Jesus. We are so intimately related to God that we need not think of God as far off, unapproachable, or unconcerned about us. We are children of God, and we can call upon him as a child calls upon his or her father.

The passage from Hebrews, with its incarnational emphases (2:14, 17), affords an opportunity to explore incarnational Christology at a moment removed from the celebration of the Nativity proper. Jesus has been born among us, and we all regard him to be fully human, at least in a formal way, as the author of this text claims. And yet, even though we say he was fully human, our emphasis on his divinity—in both formal theology and piety—seems to diminish his humanity. We stress his miracles, resurrection, and titles (Son of God, etc.), but not his limitations of birth, finitude, and mortality.

The writer of Hebrews has it right. Jesus partook of our nature (2:14), suffered (2:10, 18), and died (2:14). Yes, he was even tempted (2:18), which we hear about especially in the story of the temptation in the wilderness (Matt. 4:1–11), but which must have been a reality at other times as well. The particular temptation the wilderness story depicts is the temptation to veer from the course God had set for him. We see that temptation arise again at Gethsemane (Matt. 26:36–46).

Our Lord is the suffering, tempted, and crucified Jesus. He did not come among us as a semi-incarnate one, who traversed the earth six inches above ground, but as one who was truly incarnate. God has taken delight in the creation, in humanity, in human community, and in the individual alike. No longer need we fear death (2:15). We affirm birth and life as realities that are greater than death in power and promise. We do so because our incarnate Lord has passed from this world, through death, into the eternal world with God. Death has therefore lost its power over all humanity. It is defeated. The door has been opened for us to enter into the eternal world with God also. The Nativity of Jesus is therefore the nativity of the world, the birth of a new creation.

GOSPEL: MATTHEW 2:13–15, 19–23. The verses assigned do not contain the story of the massacre of the Holy Innocents. Since all of Matt. 2:13–23 appears to be midrashic (see the Exegesis), and not in the main historical, it is best to avoid reference to the massacre and, instead, to follow Matthew's narrative and theological emphases in a sermon.

There are two main themes: Christ in God's redemptive work and God's providential care. In regard to the first, Matthew portrays the infant Jesus as the Messiah incognito who will grow up to bring salvation. Born in Bethlehem, he was taken to Nazareth by his parents, and there he grew up. Can anything good come from there (John 1:46)? Yes, it is there that a child grew up who would be the Christ and the Redeemer. He watched farmers sow and harvest, shepherds chasing stray sheep, and craftspeople at work. He was cared for by loving parents. He was schooled in the traditions of his people, and he identified with them. In order to emphasize this point, Matthew tells a story in which the infant Jesus was taken to Egypt by his parents, and then was brought out of Egypt. That event fulfilled the words of Hosea, "Out of Egypt have I called my son" (11:1).

In the Old Testament, Israel was brought out of Egypt. That was the majestic saving act of God, setting the stage of Israel to become a redeemed and free people. The story of Jesus' coming out of Egypt points to his role in salvation too. It anticipates things to come. By his ministry, death, and resurrection, Jesus set the stage for us to become a redeemed and free people. We who belong to him participate in his exodus, his going out from this world of hostility and even crucifixion to the world of life and reconciliation.

In regard to the second theme, the story we have speaks of God's providential care for God's own. We see in the biblical story God's care of Israel, even disobedient Israel, in all times and circumstances. Matthew tells a story of God's providential care for the holy family, including the infant Jesus. Jesus was raised in a home in Nazareth and learned his father's trade (he is called "the carpenter" at Mark 6:3). He became a teacher, suffered, and was struck down at the cross. But God vindicated him in the resurrection from the dead, exalting him as Lord over the world (Matt. 28:18). So God's care for Jesus continued throughout his life and beyond it.

God's providential care extends over the creation, to each of us, throughout the globe. It extends into the parish. The biblical story of Israel and of Jesus was written to instruct us and to tell us the good news of God's providential care.

The Name of Jesus (January 1)

Lutheran	Roman Catholic	Episcopal	Common Lectionary
Num. 6:22–27	Num. 6:22–27	Exod. 34:1–8	Num. 6:22–27
Rom. 1:1–7	Gal. 4:4–7	Rom. 1:1–7	Gal. 4:4–7 or Phil. 2:9–13
Luke 2:21	Luke 2:16–21	Luke 2:15–21	Luke 2:15–21

EXEGESIS

FIRST LESSON: NUMBERS 6:22–27. The passage is located in that portion of the Book of Numbers where Israel is encamped at Mt. Sinai (1:1—10:10). Within this section there is, first of all, a census of the people according to families and tribes (1:1–54). This is followed by a process of organizing the tribes (2:1—4:49) and the institution of various ordinances (5:1—6:27). Our passage, the so-called "Priestly Blessing" or "Aaronic Benediction," comes at the end of this section of ordinances.

There is agreement among interpreters that, although the passage can be classified as Priestly (P) material, it is nevertheless considerably older than the composition of that material, coming from a traditional blessing used in worship (probably preexilic). Among its interesting features are the use of the second person singular you and its emphasis upon the divine name "Yahweh," which appears in each line of the blessing.

The opening verses (6:22–23) recount the Lord's instructions to Moses. Moses is to give the words of blessing to "Aaron and his sons," which implies that this blessing is to be used in forthcoming generations. The actual blessing is recounted in 6:24–26. It consists of three lines in the Hebrew Bible, and each contains two clauses connected by "and." The first line is the shortest (three words in Hebrew), the second is longer (five words), and the third is the longest (seven words). Whether spoken in Hebrew or English, these lines increase in rhetorical flourish as well as length. In the first line the two main verbs are "bless" and "keep" (6:24). The first verb speaks of God's bestowal of gifts, and the second of God's protection in times of trouble. Divine blessing, according to the Old Testament, brings earthly prosperity (Gen. 24:35), posterity (Gen. 28:3; Deut. 28:4), longevity (Gen. 24:1), fertility of crops and animals (Deut. 7:13–14; 28:4), and health (Deut. 7:15). The second line speaks of the Lord's making "his face to shine" upon the hearer and to "be gracious" (6:25). The imagery of a shining face is found in the Psalms (31:16; 80:3; etc.) and is associated there with God's saving work. Finally, the third line also uses the term "face" (RSV: "countenance") in clauses that can be translated, "The Lord lift up his face to you and give you peace" (6:26). That God would lift up God's face is a sign of favor, as again the Psalms attest (4:6; 44:3; 89:15). The term "peace" is a translation of the Hebrew *shalom*. While "peace" is probably the most adequate translation, the term connotes well-being and wholeness as well. Taken together, the three lines of blessing are declared to the people of Israel with the intent of effecting their content: God will provide, protect, look with favor, and bestow a sense of well-being upon God's people.

The final verse (6:27) brings the unit to a close by recalling that a command has been given—the command to pronounce this blessing. By pronouncing the blessing, the Lord's "name" is thereby put upon the people. The act signifies that the people belong to Yahweh. Furthermore, God will "bless them." This signifies (as does 6:23) that the blessing is indeed to be pronounced upon the gathered people. Yet the singular "you" within the blessing proper (6:24–26) indicates that it is pronounced for the hearing of those individuals who make up the community. Divine blessing is for the benefit of both individuals and community. One without the other is inconceivable.

The passage has both a prehistory and a posthistory. By tradition, the priests have the duty of pronouncing the divine blessing upon the people (Deut. 10:8; 21:5). This particular blessing is attested in later times (cf. Ps. 67:1; Sir. 50:20) and is of course used in worship to the present day in synagogues and churches.

SECOND LESSON: ROMANS 1:1–7 or GALATIANS 4:4–7. Concerning the passage from Romans, see the Exegesis for the Second Lesson of the Fourth Sunday in Advent. For comment on the passage from Galatians, see the Exegesis for the First Sunday after Christmas.

GOSPEL: LUKE 2:15–21. The first part of the reading (2:15–20) contains the story of the adoration of the shepherds, Mary's pondering of words and events in her heart, and the return of the shepherds to their work. These verses are discussed in the Exegesis for the Gospel for the Nativity (Luke 2:1–20).

Luke 2:21 narrates the circumcision and naming of Jesus. According to Luke's account, Mary and Joseph observe the prescriptions of the law: the circumcision of Jesus on the eighth day (Gen. 17:12; Lev. 12:3) and the purification of Mary on the fortieth (Luke 2:22; cf. Lev. 12:4). The circumcision of Jesus, as for all Jewish males, signified his formal entry into the covenant people Israel (Gen. 17:11). According to this passage, the child is named at the time of his circumcision, which is also true in the case of John the Baptist (1:59–60).

Concerning the naming of Jesus, the Prayer of the Day is an exegetical help: "Eternal Father, you gave your Son the name of Jesus to be a sign of our salvation." The name "Jesus" (English) is based on *Iēsous* (Greek), and that is found in the Septuagint for *Yehoshuah* (Hebrew), that is, Joshua. The name is a compound of Hebrew terms. Hebrew compound names, like this one, are frequently theophoric, that is, they bear the name of a god. They also, again like this one, can make statements. Well-known examples include Elijah ("Yahweh is my God") and Nathanael ("God has given" this child). The name Joshua/Jesus means either "Yahweh is salvation" or "Yahweh will save." In any case, it speaks the name of the God of Israel and of God's saving work.

In Matthew's Gospel the angel speaks the name to Joseph (and discloses its meaning to him, 1:21), and Joseph names the child (1:25). In Luke's account, however, the angel commands Mary to name the child Jesus (1:31). It is not said who gives Jesus his name on the eighth day; the passive is used, "he was called Jesus" (2:21).

The account of the circumcision and naming of Jesus portrays an observant Jewish family background for Jesus. He is subjected to the law, and he will be respectful of it (cf. 5:14; 10:26). But he will also, as "Jesus," be Savior. Luke makes much of the name of Jesus in his second volume, Acts. People are baptized into the name of Jesus (Acts 2:38; 8:16; 10:48; 19:5). But, above all, there is salvation in the name of Jesus (2:38; 4:12; 10:43; 22:16). Jesus, crucified and risen, has authority to forgive sins (as he did in his earthly ministry, Luke 5:20; 7:48; 23:34) and therefore "repentance and forgiveness of sins should be preached in his name to all nations" (Luke 24:47). In the Old Testament, Joshua brought Israel to the promised land, thereby completing the work of redemption. So Jesus will bring his people into the fullness of salvation, completing the redemptive work that God has assigned him.

HOMILETICAL INTERPRETATION

FIRST LESSON: NUMBERS 6:22–27. Perhaps the closest connection that can be made between this text, the New Testament texts, and the significance of the day is the command of God: "so shall [the priests] put my name upon the people of Israel" (6:27). By so doing, the priests enact God's claiming the people as God's own. Three consequences follow for Christian faith.

First, the name of God has been placed upon Jesus. As indicated in our exegesis of Luke 2:21, the name "Jesus" names the God of Israel. The name is actually a creedal statement that speaks of the character of this

God ("Yahweh is salvation"). The fact that Jesus bore the name of the God of Israel was a daily testimony to his belonging to this God. Although born of Mary in the fullness of time (Gal. 4:4) and raised in the home of Joseph, Jesus was incorporated into Israel through his circumcision and was named (by divine directive) to bear the name placed upon Israel for centuries through the use of the Aaronic Benediction.

Second, the divine name has been placed upon us. That is so whenever the Aaronic Benediction is used, but it is also the case because of baptism, in which the triune name of God is used as the name by which we are baptized. The circumcision and naming of Jesus have parallels in the traditional ceremony of christening, which has included both baptizing and naming the child. But the most important connection is that in baptism we are incorporated into Christ, thereby sharing in his destiny of death and new life (Rom. 6:1–11), and through him belong to the triune God (Matt. 28:19).

Third, the God who is named seeks our good. God continues to care for all that he has made and provides sustenance for all things *(creatio continua),* as we are reminded by Jesus in his discourse against anxiety in the Sermon on the Mount (Matt. 6:25–33; cf. 5:45). Whenever the Aaronic Benediction is used, we hear the good news that God will provide for us all that is needful as we go on our way. Although the benediction may well be the closing act of a service of worship, it does not mark the close of our dealings with God or vice versa. It is precisely in our taking leave of the service that God's presence and work for our good are declared to be realities.

SECOND LESSON: ROMANS 1:1–7 or GALATIANS 4:4–7. For homiletical interpretations of these passages, see those for the Fourth Sunday in Advent and the First Sunday after Christmas, respectively.

GOSPEL: LUKE 2:15–21. We are so accustomed to the name given to the child of Mary that we attach no special significance to it. True, it is seldom used as a name for anyone other than Jesus of Nazareth and so it has special significance in that sense. But generally we take it as just a name.

But the name given to Jesus sums up two features about him. First, it anticipates and sets forth the message that Jesus was to proclaim: "The Lord is salvation." Even if that message is not replicated word for word in chapter and verse in our Gospels, it is the core of his proclamation. His summons to repentance, to faith, and into the kingdom of God were predicated on his prior claim that the God of Israel and of the whole world was a saving God, a God who despised nothing that he had made, a God who is ever seeking to embrace his creation in love. So too the miracles of Jesus were saving acts by which God was at work in and through him to restore the hurt and the ill; they were acts of healing (salvation).

Second, the name given to Jesus not only speaks of Jesus' own message, but sets forth a message about Jesus. His coming into the world was a saving action of God. After his career was over—after his crucifixion and resurrection—his followers proclaimed Jesus as God's salvation, the Savior. They preached, baptized, and forgave sins in his name (see Exegesis).

We have in the naming of Jesus (as "Jesus") one of those grand coincidental events of history—or is it the guiding of God, even as the Scriptures declare? The name fits. This is sometimes true of persons generally (an Ernest can often be quite earnest), and we wonder how they could possibly have any other names than those given. In the case of Jesus, the name speaks of both the message he proclaims and the career he fulfills (the work he does).

Some fine hymns about the name of Jesus can be drawn upon for homiletical material or congregational singing. These include "Jesus, Name of Wondrous Love" by William W. How, "Jesus, Name All Names Above" by Theoctistus of the Stadium, and "Jesus, the Very Thought of You" by Bernard of Clairvaux.

The Second Sunday after Christmas

Lutheran	Roman Catholic	Episcopal	Common Lectionary
Isa. 61:10—62:3	Sir. 24:1–2, 8–12	Jer. 31:7–14	Jer. 31:7–14 or Ecclus. 24:1–4, 12–16
Eph. 1:3–6, 15–18	Eph. 1:3–6, 15–18	Eph. 1:3–6, 15–19a	Eph. 1:3–6, 15–18
John 1:1–18	John 1:1–18	Matt. 2:13–15, 19–23	John 1:1–18

EXEGESIS

FIRST LESSON: ISAIAH 61:10—62:3 or JEREMIAH 31:7–14. The Isaiah passage belongs to the third portion of the book (Isaiah 56–66), commonly called Trito-Isaiah and regarded as postexilic in origin. Both parts of the passage (61:10–11 and 62:1–3) speak of the salvation of

Jerusalem (or Zion). Earlier in Isaiah 61 there are references to the rebuilding of Jerusalem after the exile (61:4), its prosperity (61:6), and the restoration of its honor (61:7). Now in 61:10–11 it is as though the city itself is speaking praises to God for salvation. The reasons for rejoicing are stated in two major assertions introduced by the word "for" *(ki* in Hebrew). The first (61:10; notice "for" in the third line of the RSV text) is God's saving work; the second (61:11) is the certainty that God's saving work will be made evident to all people. The parallel imagery in 61:10 of being clothed with garments and covered with a robe establishes the conceptual parallelism of salvation and righteousness. God's salvation is God's victory, shared with God's people; God's righteousness is the disposition and power to set matters right, to vindicate God's people. And as surely as the earth produces vegetation, so "the Lord will cause righteousness and praise" to be prominent in all the world (61:11). Righteousness will prevail in all relationships—among people, and in their relationship to God—and all the nations will take notice.

In the second part of our passage (62:1–3) the prophet no longer impersonates the city but speaks concerning it and, at the same time, to it (see "you" in 62:2–3). He expects the complete vindication of the city: "vindication . . . as brightness," "salvation as a burning torch." Indeed, the vindication will be so obvious and public that "the nations" and "all the kings" will see it (62:2a). The "new name" that will be given (62:2b) would not be a replacement for the traditional one (Jerusalem). Rather, the naming of the city has to do with its identity before God (cf. also Isa. 1:26; Jer. 33:16 for name changes). This becomes clear in 62:4 (which is not a part of our reading) where the switching of names is made: no longer does the city bear the label "Forsaken" *(Azubah)* but has the name "my delight is in her" *(Hephzibah).* In the final verse (62:3) the prophet declares that the city of Jerusalem will enjoy splendor (as a "crown of beauty") and power (as a "royal diadem").

The reading reflects major themes of Third Isaiah in the postexilic era. The return from the exile (538 B.C. and later) was considered an act of divine deliverance, and it was for a purpose. The prophet expects that God will restore the fortunes of the people, and that this will have universal effects, culminating in the worship and service of God, not by Israel alone, but by all the nations (66:18). The vindication of Jerusalem is a step in the process, and along with that is right worship and righteousness among all the people (60:21; 61:6, 8; 65:7; 66:2).

The passage from Jeremiah (31:7–14) forms a unit unto itself apart from its surrounding context. It rejoices in Israel's homecoming from exile and must have been composed either late in the time of exile (587–539 B.C.) or soon thereafter. Its first part (31:7–9) portrays the joyful return of scattered Israelites into their homeland, including those with misfortune or distress (31:8). Their return is eased by topographical transformations, a theme reminiscent of Isa. 35:1–10 (Advent 3). The second part (31:10–14) portrays the restoration of the people in idyllic terms. The Lord is spoken of as a shepherd (cf. Isa. 40:11; Ezek. 34:12). The basis for such secure imagery about God is that God has "ransomed" or "redeemed" (31:11) Jacob (= Israel), that is, delivered God's people from captivity (cf. Isa. 48:20). This people can now expect further blessings in the land, as well as the joy and merriment of a new era of freedom (31:12–13). Both priests and the people at large will be abundantly satisfied (31:14). The picture is one of perfect contentment.

SECOND LESSON: EPHESIANS 1:3–6, 15–18.   The Epistle to the Ephesians is widely regarded in critical scholarship as deutero-Pauline (i.e., written by someone of a Pauline school after the death of Paul himself), and that will be assumed here. Our lesson is from an opening doxology (1:3–14) and the thanksgiving section (1:15–23).

The doxological portion of our lesson (1:3–6) presents us immediately with the writer's nexus of Christology and cosmology. For him, Christ is "in the heavenly places" (1:3), ruling over the cosmos (cf. 1:20). The "heavenly places" are at the same time the final destiny of the redeemed. To these people "every spiritual blessing" located in the heavenly places has been imparted already "in Christ" (understood in an instrumental sense, i.e., "by means of Christ"), although complete realization is future—an inheritance (1:14, 18). The next two verses (1:4–5) speak of God's election (Greek: *exelexatō;* RSV: "he chose us") and predestination (Greek: *proorisas;* RSV: "he destined us"). According to the writer, God's election of Christians was (1) "in him" (= Christ) and (2) "before the foundation of the world." The language is doxological, and what it says is that the redeeming God known in Christ has intended to have a people since eternity. (One should not press the passage literally, so that it implies that God's election of certain persons took place temporally before Adam's fall.) The purpose of God's election, an act of love (1:5a), is that God might have children (RSV: "sons") through Christ, that is, children reconciled to God. All of this results properly in "the praise of his glorious grace" which has been bestowed in "the Beloved" (Christ, who is called God's "beloved Son" at his baptism; cf. Mark 1:11 par.). That God is an electing God is in keeping with Old Testament traditions concerning God's election of Israel (Exod. 19:4–6; Deut. 7:7; 23:5; Amos 3:2, etc.). It is also in keeping with Paul's view that God has called him and others through the gospel to create and fashion a people of the new age (Rom. 10:14–17; 11:1–6). God does this electing not for privileges for the elect, but in order that his saving work might be accomplished.

The thanksgiving portion (1:15–18) uses characteristic terminology and recalls similar passages in the genuine Pauline letters (e.g., Rom. 1:8–18). The writer expresses his thanks for his recipient's "faith in the Lord Jesus" and their "love toward all the saints." The two items (with some verbatim similarities) are also recounted in Col. 1:4. The author goes on to speak of his wish for his readers, and that for which he prays: that God might give them a spirit of wisdom and revelation in the knowledge of himself (1:17). The term "spirit" here must mean "state of mind" or "disposition" (as in "spirit of your mind," Eph. 4:23; "spirit of gentleness," 1 Cor. 4:21); the effect would then be to have a disposition of receptivity to wisdom and revelation, which provide knowledge (or insight, as the term means in Greek) of God. Such knowledge enlightens the eyes of one's heart (1:18)—a beautiful mix of metaphors indeed! The believer thus "sees" with the eyes of faith; he or she knows what the Christian "hope" is (1:19). As elsewhere in Scripture, "hope" does not mean wishful thinking (as in hope for good weather), but certainty. The content of Christian hope is the "glorious inheritance" in store for the "saints." A person is called to that hope by God through the proclamation of the gospel. The author does not imply that his readers lack the knowledge and hope spoken of in this passage (for they have heard the gospel and have been "enlightened" already, 1:13, 15, 18). Rather, he uses the typical feature of thanksgiving sections to provide hints of what is coming later in the letter. The letter goes on to share insights into the mysteries of God and the Christian hope, particularly in regard to the breaking down of barriers between Jew and gentile (cf. 2:14), so that gentiles have a share in the inheritance of the saints, the Christian hope.

GOSPEL: JOHN 1:1–18. The prologue to the Gospel of John is generally regarded as a combination of poetry and prose. Accordingly, it is said that there are three stanzas of poetry (1:1–5; 1:9–13; 1:14, 16–18) and two prose interruptions (1:6–8; 1:15).

The prose sections speak about John the Baptist. They need little comment here except to say that they serve to put John into his place as a witness to the Christ, thus showing how it was that many of John's disciples came to be Christians (i.e., John himself led them to Jesus), or perhaps polemicizing against a still extant Baptist sect—or both.

The poetic sections are of more interest and importance. It is widely held that these three stanzas are from a hymn that has been attached secondarily to the Gospel of John by an editor (redactor) of the Johannine school—a view that is adopted here. An exegetical advantage to understanding the material in this way is that we do not have to try to figure out how it can be narrating a sequence of events; rather, we can understand it as celebrating three aspects of the "career" of the *logos* (Word). The passage surely does not narrate a sequence of events, for the affirmation that "the Word became flesh" (1:14) comes later in the prologue than do the statements made earlier about his being in the world and coming to his own people (1:10–12). If we set the prose portions aside, we are left with a hymn of three stanzas, and as in a triptych the second dominates the set of three, but at the same time it cannot stand alone. Each stanza speaks of an aspect of the life and work of the *logos:*

1. Cosmic existence of the *logos* prior to history and active in creation (1:1–4)
2. Earthly appearance of the *logos* in history and its rejection and acceptance in the world (1:9–13)
3. Communal legacy of the *logos* in the church and its gifts of grace and truth (1:14, 16–18)

The first of these stanzas affirms that the entire cosmos has been created "through" or "by means of" Christ, the *logos*. There is no hint of the Fall. Yet it is presupposed in the second stanza, which affirms that the earthly ministry of the *logos* in Jesus was redemptive, a means by which the fallen creation was restored in those who believe. And the third stanza affirms the existence of a community of believers ("we" being used for the first time) that belongs to the new creation, the fruits of Christ's redemptive work.

The passage sets forth in one place the clearest claims of the New Testament concerning Christ's preexistence, work in creation, and incarnation. Behind such thinking is the Jewish wisdom tradition. God's wisdom *(sophia)* is personified in Prov. 8:22–31, and she speaks there of her presence with God as an agent in the creation of the universe. In the Wisdom of Solomon, wisdom *(sophia)* and the word *(logos)* of God are identified as one, and this *sophia/logos* is instrumental in creation (9:1–2). The writer of the prologue to John's Gospel is therefore not an innovator in speaking of a preexistent *logos* that has a role in creation. What is new is the author's claim that the *logos* has become incarnate in Jesus of Nazareth. Of course, the term *logos* is also to be found in non-Jewish Hellenistic thought and literature, especially in Stoicism, referring to the rational principle of the universe. The author's words at the opening of the prologue thus speak potentially to an even wider circle of understanding. The claim of the incarnation of the *logos* in Jesus of Nazareth, however, would be an innovation here as well.

That Christ (the *logos*) has a role in creation signifies that what one associates with him in his historical ministry has been characteristic of God from the beginning. That is that the universe has been created by a God whose love and care extend outward to all things, establishing a "place" and dignity even for the weak and the rejected. Nothing was made without the *logos* (1:13). Yet the primary purpose of the stanza is to glorify Christ. He is the one in whom there is "life," which is identified here as "the light" of human beings. Life and light can be identified metaphorically when they are understood to be the particular spiritual quality that Christ brings—the authentic life of the children of God—to those who hear and believe the gospel, and thus gain eternal life (5:24) and the illumination that guides them away from darkness and death (8:12; 12:35–36).

Yet the earthly existence of the *logos*—personified in the ministry of Jesus of Nazareth—causes division in the world (1:9–13). The world by itself tends toward darkness (3:19), and the Gospel of John shall go on to portray the world's rejection of Jesus. The "world" for this evangelist is hostile to both Christ and his followers (7:7; 15:18–19; 17:14). The "true light" came into the world in order to save it from the darkness of its unbelief. Yet the world did not recognize this light in Jesus. Although at 1:11 the RSV reads, "he came to his own home," which could imply Nazareth of Galilee, the Greek text simply says, "he came to his own (*idia*)," which can signify the created sphere, but "his own (*idioi*)"— which will mean human beings—rejected him. Nevertheless, there is a community within the created sphere that has received the light (1:12); they are the "children of God," reconciled to God and possessing life from the Christ. They are "born . . . of God" (RSV, 1:13) or "by God" (cf. 3:3) for the life God intends for them. This life cannot be obtained by human efforts. It is totally a gift from God, as one's natural life is a gift of one's parents.

The communal legacy of the *logos,* which is the focus of the third stanza (1:14, 16–18), is predicated on the incarnation (1:14). Although the Son has returned to the Father, he is remembered by the community as having come in human flesh among human beings. He revealed the Father ("we beheld his glory") and was truly "full of grace and truth." The phrase "grace upon grace" (1:16) can mean simply an abundance of grace—grace flowing continuously. The juxtaposition of law through Moses and grace and truth through Christ in 1:17 does not necessarily denigrate the law. God's gifts have been given both through Moses (the law) and through Christ (grace and truth), and the latter exceed the former in splendor, for they are the means to life abundant in this world and beyond ("eternal life"). The passage ends with the ringing declaration that the Son (RSV) alone has revealed God in the world (1:18). There are text-critical problems with this verse. Where the RSV reads "the only Son," there is sound textual support (adopted by the Nestle-Aland Greek text, 26th ed.) for "[the] only begotten God" or (better in English) "God, the only begotten." In light of 1:1, where the *logos* is declared to be God, this rendering is possible theologically (cf. also 20:28), and the textual evidence surely favors it. In any case, it is a major Johannine theme that Christ came from the Father and revealed the Father in the world (10:38; 12:45; 13:3; 14:9).

HOMILETICAL INTERPRETATION

FIRST LESSON: ISAIAH 61:10—62:3 or JEREMIAH 31:7–14. The Isaiah passage relates to the season at three places in particular. The first is the promise that the Lord will cause "righteousness and praise to spring forth before all the nations" (61:11). This promise, for Christian faith, has been confirmed in Jesus Christ, whose birth has been celebrated. He is the one who brings righteousness into the world through his ministry and by means of his sacrificial death for others. This is brought out particularly in Paul's Letter to the Romans, where he says that God's righteousness has been revealed in Jesus Christ (3:22). Specifically, the atoning death of Jesus on the cross is a demonstration of God's righteousness, God's establishing of a right relationship between the world and God. Indeed, Paul says that God made Jesus to be "our wisdom, our righteousness and sanctification and redemption" (1 Cor. 1:30).

The expectation of the prophet is that the advent of righteousness will be "before the nations." In Jesus we have, says Simeon, a salvation "prepared in the presence of all people, a light for revelation to the Gentiles, and for glory to [God's] people Israel" (Luke 2:30–32). Though born of Mary and of the house of Israel, the Righteous One is the Redeemer of the world. Besides the connection to the song of Simeon, a connection can also be made between Isa. 61:10 and the Song of Mary (the Magnificat, Luke 1:46–55). The first two lines of each are strikingly similar.

The second way that the Isaiah passage fits the time of year is in its anticipation of Epiphany. The words of 62:2 ("The nations shall see your vindication, and all the kings your glory") can hardly be read without picturing in one's mind the visit of the Magi (even though they were not kings), the manifestation of the Christ to the gentiles ("nations" and "gentiles" represent the same word in Hebrew, as also in Greek).

Finally, the closing words of 62:2 ("and you shall be called by a new name which the mouth of the Lord will give") recall the naming of Jesus according to the Lord's command through an angel (Luke 1:31; 2:21). He is given a name that speaks of his saving work (see the Exegesis and Homiletical Interpretation for the Luke text for the Name of Jesus), and those who are baptized in his name become beneficiaries of the salvation he brings.

The alternate reading (Jer. 31:7–14) has associations with the Christmas Season at several points: "The Lord has saved his people" (31:7), the reference to the woman with child coming from the north country (31:8, which can suggest the trek of Mary and Joseph from Nazareth to Bethlehem), and the reference to Ephraim (Israel) as the Lord's "first-born" (31:9). But once the verbal associations are seen, it is questionable whether they should be pressed. A sermon on this text might better explore its imagery of hope, and then proclaim the good news that the deepest longings and hopes of the human heart and mind have been fulfilled in the Christ event, which we celebrate in this season. The well-known canticle, "Listen! You Nations" *(Lutheran Book of Worship,* 14), is based on this text and could be incorporated into the service.

SECOND LESSON: EPHESIANS 1:3–6, 15–18. The first portion of the passage has to do with election, and the second speaks of enlightenment. A sermon might be devoted to an explication of the meaning of election alone or election and enlightenment. It would be more difficult to focus only on enlightenment, since it presupposes election here. Moreover, while the gospel can be heard in connection with election, it is less likely to be heard in a sermon on enlightenment.

As explicated in our exegesis above, God is understood by biblical writers as an electing God. Christians of the present day may or may not think of themselves as elect. Here is a good place to put the law/gospel dialectic to work. Some who think of themselves as the elect—on the grounds that they are church members, Americans, or whatever—may need to be reminded that when Israel arrogated to itself such thinking, but failed to draw from it the consequences for worship and conduct, prophetic judgment often followed. On the other hand, Christians ought to hear the good news about God's working through election. God is an electing God for the sake of saving the world. The elect are those who witness to the reality and power of God. So God called Israel into being, and ever since the apostolic age God has been calling people through the gospel, by the work of the Spirit, into a community of faith and witness, the church.

But the elect belong to a dynamic fellowship, and they are (or ought to be) constantly on the way to a greater understanding of God. Although there is a great deal of anti-intellectualism in our culture, which manifests itself above all in matters of faith, it has not always and everywhere been so. The writer attests to this in his wish that his readers will obtain "a spirit of wisdom and of revelation in the knowledge of [God]" (1:17) and enlightenment (1:18). The history of the church is replete with persons who have grown in faith and in their understanding of God and the dynamics of faith and witness in the world. In our time, however, it seems that growth is not encouraged. A colleague once remarked, "We teach children and bless adults. Jesus blessed children and taught adults." There is truth in that observation. The quest for spirituality by adults in our time could be a symptom of our failure as pastors and teachers to offer them a robust and vital vision of faith and discipleship. Jesus did not call people to spirituality, but to faith and discipleship.

Growth in one's understanding of God and the life of faith comes in different ways to different people—and even for the same person. The apostle Paul, for example, learned and grew in understanding from his study of the Scriptures (Old Testament) in rabbinical school, but also in his experience of the "thorn in the flesh" (2 Cor. 12:7–10). Our own growth in faith and the knowledge of God takes place as we worship, study, pray, talk with others about life's issues, and interpret our experience (good and bad) in the light of our Christian heritage. All this must be done, however, in a spirit of openness that affirms the presence and goodness of God. There are no heretical questions, and orthodox answers do not exist for every question.

Election and enlightenment are joined in our text, and they should be joined in our time. God calls, or elects, a people to be a community of witness in the world. The witness of this community, to be credible, must be wise, founded on the knowledge of God.

GOSPEL: JOHN 1:1–18.   It is fitting, indeed desirable, that this great text have a hearing at some point in the Christmas Season. The Nativity text of Luke 2:1–20 is the more popular, and it always gets a hearing, but the prologue to John is more substantial. Planning for worship on this day calls for packing away "O Little Town of Bethlehem" for another year and bringing out "Of the Father's Love Begotten."

The text touches upon many topics: creation, revelation, the preexistence of Christ, redemption, the incarnation, Christology (especially the humanity and divinity of Christ, and the relationship between the Son and the Father), regeneration, and more. A sermon based on it will most likely focus upon the incarnation, the appearance of the *logos* in history (see Exegesis). But it should be borne in mind that the incarnation in the Johannine sense concerns the ministry of the adult Jesus (who was both received and rejected, 1:11–12), not his birth itself.

How can one illustrate the incarnation of the Word? One way is to start out with some basic thoughts about the word "word." A word can be a particular oral or written syllable or polysyllable; "if," "and," and "but" are words. But the word "word" can have a broader meaning. It can refer to a statement or expression (which is true of the word *logos* as well), as in the statements, "His word is always good" or "You have my word on it."

When the writer of the prologue therefore speaks of Christ as the eternal and preexistent Word of God, he is saying, among other things, that Christ is the eternal expression of God. He is the one who "articulates" for God in the creation of the world. Further, this eternal expression of God has also been "articulated" within our world, within human history, in Jesus of Nazareth. Jesus is the enfleshment (incarnation) of what God wants to say. God is invested, clothed, in Jesus as God's expression to us.

The purpose of this investment—God's utterance taking on human flesh—is revelatory and soteriological. God is revealed in Jesus as in no other way. No longer can we say that God is unknown. The mystery of God is not diminished, but all that one could possibly know in this world about God's nature is disclosed as fully as possible (cf. 1:18). Yet the incarnation was not simply a means of revelation. In the final analysis, humanity needs a Savior, not just a Revealer. Jesus is both. The good news of the prologue is that Christ has given us "power to become children of God" through faith (1:12). This is possible because the Son has "power over all flesh, to give eternal life to all whom [the Father] has given him" (17:2). As God's agent of redemption, Jesus is able to do as he wishes, and that is to give life to men, women, and children—the authentic life of the children of God.

The response of the church to this good news of revelation and redemption is to glorify God, doxology. In the Gospel of Luke, the Gloria in Excelsis serves this purpose (2:14), as it does in the worship of the church to this day. The doxology of the Johannine community is enclosed in the third stanza of the prologue (1:14, 16–18). Though it is not sung in the church today as a hymn, its lines could be printed for recitation by the congregation following the sermon or at some other appropriate place in the service.